6/06

CHRISTINE L. WILLIAMS

WORKING, SHOPPING, AND SOCIAL INEQUALITY

UNIVERSITY OF CALIFORNIA PRESS
Berkeley   Los Angeles   London

University of California Press, one of the most distinguished
university presses in the United States, enriches lives around
the world by advancing scholarship in the humanities, social
sciences, and natural sciences. Its activities are supported by
the UC Press Foundation and by philanthropic
contributions from individuals and institutions. For more
information, visit www.ucpress.edu.

An earlier version of chapter 3 appeared in *Qualitative Sociology* 27, no. 4 (2004): 461–86. Used with kind permission of
Springer Science and Business Media.

University of California Press
Berkeley and Los Angeles, California

University of California Press, Ltd.
London, England

© 2006 by The Regents of the University of California

Library of Congress Cataloging-in-Publication Data

Williams, Christine L., 1959–.
Inside toyland : working, shopping, and social inequality /
Christine L. Williams.
p.   cm.
Includes bibliographical references and index.
ISBN 0-520-24716-7 (cloth : alk. paper) —
ISBN 0-520-24717-5 (pbk. : alk. paper)
1. Toy industry—United States—Employees. 2. Clerks (Re-
tail trade)—United States. 3. Discrimination in employ-
ment—United States. 4. Consumers—United States. 5.
Equality—United States. I. Title.

HD8039.T672U68   2006
381'.4568872'0973—dc22   2005006565

Manufactured in the United States of America

14   13   12   11   10   09   08   07   06
10   9   8   7   6   5   4   3   2   1

The paper used in this publication meets
the minimum requirements of
ANSI/NISO Z39.48–1992 (R 1997) (*Permanence of Paper*).

For my parents, Bunnie and Clyde Williams;

my sisters, Cathie Holland and Karrie Williams;

and my grandparents, Valentyna and Stanislaw Swiatek

and Elizabeth and Clyde Williams

CONTENTS

ACKNOWLEDGMENTS

I started this project when I was on sabbatical leave from my job at the University of Texas at Austin. A number of my colleagues there helped me and inspired me. I trace my original interest in children and youth culture to my former graduate students Rana Emerson and Kristen Schilt. Debra Umberson and Chandra Muller supported this project in a most fundamental way by agreeing to act as references for my job applications and expressing great enthusiasm for the project. Dana Britton offered her usual unstinting and constructive criticism, as did Kirsten Dellinger and Jeff Jackson. Gretchen Ritter, Janet Staiger, Julie Reid, Gretchen Webber, and Rob Crosnoe are among my many other colleagues at Texas who encouraged and publicized my work.

A surprising number of non-Texans also contributed to this work. Mike Messner, Sherryl Kleinman, and Viviana Zelizer helped me to organize and clarify my thoughts by inviting me to give talks at conferences and by offering excellent advice. Allison Pugh and Robert Zussman pushed me to think in new directions and to write more clearly; I hope they will see their influence throughout the text as much as I do. Sarah Banet-Weiser, Barrie Thorne, Neil Smelser, Dan Cook, Amy Hanser, Nicholas Hoover Wilson, and especially Naomi Schneider provided helpful feedback at various stages. The book is better because of them.

I've also enjoyed talking about this project with many friends, including Ricardo Gonzalez (who has taught me a lot about shopping), Ward and Dee Bell, Bob Freeland, and Jodi Lerner (who came up with the magnificently apt pseudonym Diamond Toys).

My mother and sisters did their part by clipping stories from newspapers and magazines. They also made me pay attention to the pleasures of shopping (but still I prefer tennis with Dad). And thanks especially to Martin Button. Retail work is exhausting, and I would come home from an eight-hour shift to face another three hours in front of the computer writing field notes. I couldn't have done it without Martin's constant reassurance, calming influence, and overall Zenlike approach to life. Thank you.

1

A SOCIOLOGIST INSIDE TOY STORES

I got my first job working in a toy store when I was forty-one years old. I called the Toy Warehouse[1] to ask if they were hiring, and the manager, Olive, invited me to come in and fill out a computer application. Someone else was using the computer when I arrived at the store, but after waiting for fifteen minutes I got my chance. The computer asked when I was available to work (any time!) and if I was willing to take a drug test (of course!), then administered a twenty-five-item multiple-choice personality test. Each question gave four statements or words, and I was supposed to choose the ones that best described me and that least described me. For instance: Was I friendly, aggressive, opinionated, or meek? Leader, follower, competitive, or nice? When I had finished, the computer instructed me to obtain a printout of my record from the service desk. I did that and was then escorted to a little cubbyhole of an office, where I met Olive, an extremely overweight African American woman about my age.

There was absolute chaos in that tiny office, a condition I would come to regard as normal at the store. It was a mess of papers, boxes, and toys. The phone was ringing and people were knocking on the door. An emergency had arisen—an unscheduled delivery—and the staff needed the forklift to unload the truck, but no one knew where the keys were and who, if anyone, was qualified to operate it. Olive was being asked to resolve this situation as she was trying to interview me.

Olive told me she wanted to hire motivated sellers who could provide excellent customer service. Although I didn't have any retail experience, I told her I knew I could do the job. Olive put three toys in front of me: a CD cartridge of a Lara Croft Tomb Raider video game, a white Barbie in a bikini packaged inside a sand pail to take to the beach, and a black Barbie dressed in a seventies outfit. She said, "Pick one and sell it to me."

I took a long breath. In my other life I am a professor of sociology who specializes in gender and sexuality studies. Barbie has become a symbol of the postmodernist turn in gender studies; her cultural meaning has been deconstructed and reconstructed by a number of feminist theorists (Lord 1994; McDonough 1999; Rand 1995). I devote an entire section of my course on sexuality to unpacking Barbie's significance. But far from being helpful, those arguments almost paralyzed me. The complex race and gender politics of the situation—a white woman selling a black or a white Barbie to Olive—were simply overwhelming.

I said, "Well, you don't have to sell Barbie; girls always want her" (mentioning that I had read that the average ten-year-old girl owns eight of the dolls), "so I will sell you the CD." Lara Croft is not exactly a wholesome or apolitical alternative to Barbie. One of the earliest female icons of computer gaming, her long flowing hair, enormous breasts, and crack fighting skills set the standard for the dozens of imitators that followed. I said that if we assumed that Olive had a PlayStation she needed this game because it was the basis for a movie that had just opened (starring

Angelina Jolie). Olive asked me if the product was new. I made a guess and said no, but it was a good choice if she didn't already have it. I also said that it was important for girls to be computer literate; as long as the parents approved of the content, girls should be exposed to the same computer games as boys so they could compete in the real world.

Then Olive shook my hand and told me that I had the job.

THE SOCIOLOGY OF SHOPPING

Sociologists have not had much to say about the business of toy selling, or indeed about any kind of selling.[2] For the most part, we have ceded the study of buying and selling to economists. In this book I make the case for a specifically sociological approach to shopping. Decisions regarding where to buy, how to buy, and what to buy are shaped by a complex of social, cultural, and psychological factors that sociologists are well equipped to analyze. Furthermore, I will argue that these consumer choices contribute to social inequality.

The connection between shopping and inequality begins with the decision of *where* to buy. Consumers make choices to enter one store and not another based in part on the images projected in advertisements. Corporate retail executives develop marketing plans, store designs, and labor policies to appeal to a certain kind of customer, or at least to a certain kind of customer desire, such as the desire for status or for low prices. Gender, race, and class distinctions all enter into the formation of this corporate image. Inside the store, corporate agendas are implemented in ways that favor certain groups over others. Workers are sorted into an organizational hierarchy and assigned specific duties according to their race, gender, and class. These internal practices shape *how* we buy: they determine with whom customers interact inside the store, which customers receive attentive service, and who ultimately benefits from the social norms that guide these interactions. The social inequalities of shopping are also taught to children, a practice especially apparent inside a toy store. Both in the style of interacting and in decisions about *what* to buy, adults instruct children on the values and meanings of consumerism, which contain lessons about race, class, and gender.

Throughout this book, I explain how shopping reproduces social inequality. But I also emphasize that this connection is not seamless or uncontested. Collective actions, on the part of both workers and consumer groups, have challenged these social inequalities of shopping in the past. I argue that more of these actions are needed today.

Sociology hasn't always been silent about shopping. In the early days of the profession at the turn of the twentieth century, when sociology was more closely allied with social work and progressivism, women sociologists turned their attention to the plight of retail workers. Leisure shopping, like sociology, was a relatively new phenomenon. Department stores, the first "palaces of consumption" (Benson 1986, 82), opened in the late 1800s and by the 1920s became popular urban destinations for middle- and upper-class women. These early stores were modeled after fancy private clubs. They offered a range of luxurious services to flatter the pretensions of the haute bourgeoisie. In addition to offering a rich, aesthetically pleasurable environment for meeting with friends, many stores provided nurseries, valet parking, delivery services, doormen, restaurants, public lectures, and even baths. But the indulgences offered to the customers were not matched by a similar generosity toward the stores' saleswomen. Benson writes that store managers were originally inclined to treat sales workers as factory workers; it took several decades before they tailored their labor practices specifically for service work. The greater visibility of service work compared to factory work made these practices open to public scrutiny, attracting the attentions of sociologists and other reform-minded progressives. Benson writes, "Women shoppers were outraged at seeing overworked, underpaid women toil long hours in unhealthy surroundings; almost invariably the same middle- and upper-class women who made up the backbone of the store's clientele spearheaded the campaigns for better conditions for working women" (128). Among the organizations involved in the fight for better working conditions for retail workers were the National Consumers' League, the Women's Trade Union League, and the Young Women's Christian Association (134).

Sociologists helped by documenting the conditions of these workers, sometimes through participant observation, as in the case of Annie Marion MacLean.[3] MacLean, who was a member of the Consumers' League and affiliated with Hull House (the famous settlement house founded by Jane Addams), spent two weeks working in Chicago department stores during the 1898 Christmas season. Her goal was to document the working conditions of women and children retail workers from the inside. As she wrote, "Employers are always ready to tell the best conditions that exist; it remains to others to find the worst" (MacLean 1899, 722). MacLean believed that if the public were confronted with firsthand information on stores' hours, pay, and working conditions, the stores would be forced to clean up their acts. If they refused, they could be sanctioned by the Consumers' League, which "utterly refuses to indorse [sic] stores that do not live up to its standard all the time."

Annie MacLean applied for several jobs during the Christmas rush and ended up getting two, both in the toy sections of large department stores. In two weeks, she worked 175 hours and earned a grand total of $11.88, or, as she computes it, "a little more than six cents an hour" (738). Her account of her experiences was published as the lead article in the *American Journal of Sociology* in 1899. In that article, "Two Weeks in Department Stores," she describes the financial hardships she experienced trying to live on this income and documents the plight of other saleswomen in similar jobs. She also recounts her trying interactions with managers, who often terrorized the workers and did little to relieve their suffering:

> One day a manager of the stores appeared on our floor, and in ringing tones called out "424!" [MacLean's employee number]. As I was starting to answer the summons, my young friend threw her arms around me and said: "Don't you mind Tom Jones, he can't hurt you. Tell him you're a new girl, if he scolds you; and if he's ugly, tell him to go to h——." I did not do any of these things, and I got away unhurt. He had no grievance against me, but he had such a rude way of addressing the clerks that they were all afraid of him. (732)

Customer interactions were equally fraught. Shoppers were demanding, unsympathetic, patronizing, and rude. MacLean wrote:

> A man made me open and take the dolls from nineteen boxes to see if I could not find him one with black eyes and yellow hair. I told him they were all gone, at the price he desired, but he wanted me to verify my statement. As if it would mat-

ter to his two-year-old baby whether the doll had black or green eyes! He was evidently buying one for his own delectation. That is only one instance of the many exacting customers we met. (735)

Many shoppers treated MacLean with condescension and disdain, others with patronizing concern. Some insisted on inquiring about workers' wages, causing MacLean to wonder "just why saleswomen should be subjected to such rudeness by seemingly intelligent people" (733).

MacLean's article ends with an appeal to "intelligent and educated people" to support the work of the Consumers' League. She argues that consumers have a responsibility not to shop in stores that do not treat workers properly and to support legislation to protect workers' rights to fair wages, hours, and working conditions:

> So long as the consumer will patronize bad stores, so long will they exist; so long as people will buy clothing produced under inhuman conditions, so long will they continue to be produced under just those conditions. Has the public no duty in the matter? . . . Inhuman and demoralizing conditions must be removed. Some of the evils here could be speedily remedied by legislation and faithful inspection. Those who have not already considered the matter would do well to peruse carefully the Consumers' standard of a fair house, and ask themselves whether or not they can do something to lessen the hardships of the salespeople's lives. (740)

A little over a century after Annie MacLean's department store experience, I spent three months—a total of more than three hundred hours—working as a clerk in two toy stores. Like MacLean,

I undertook this study to investigate the social conditions of retail work, no longer one of the newest but now one of the largest and fastest-growing occupations in the service sector of the U.S. economy. Both of us were motivated by an interest in enhancing the lives of women service workers. But unlike MacLean, who couched her concerns in the protectionist rhetoric of the day, I was interested in the issues of equal opportunities and worker rights in this industry.

It is a case of pure serendipity that we both ended up selling toys. When I went to work in the toy store, I didn't know about Annie MacLean's study.[4] I chose to study toy stores because, although their merchandise is discretionary (unlike, say, that of grocery stores), they attract a wide range of customers. Interacting with customers is a central part of the retail worker's job, and I wanted the chance to observe the age, race, ethnicity, gender, and class differences among shoppers. Further, because children often accompany adults while shopping for toys, the toy store provides a window into the socialization of the next generation of consumers. Finally, toy stores are interesting to me because—as I was reminded in my job interview with Olive—toys can be a significant source of gender socialization for children.[5]

One of the toy stores where I worked I call the Toy Warehouse. It was located in the outskirts of an urban area in a redevelopment zone. It was what is sometimes called a big box store and was surrounded by several others, such as Home Depot, OfficeMax, and Petsmart. An enormous parking lot spread out like a lake between the stores. There were no sidewalks, no trees, no benches. Customers drove their cars to a specific store and then drove to another one if they wished to continue their shopping.

Some of my fellow employees told me that workers in other

Toy Warehouses referred to our store as "the hood," referring to the "bad neighborhood" that surrounded it. As one of my co-workers said, "They think they can put a store anywhere and it will be OK, but face it, we are in the middle of a ghetto. It may look like a suburban shopping mall, but it's located in one of the worst areas." It was well known that our store had the worst problem with "shrink" (what retailers call theft) in the entire region. We also had the worst customer satisfaction rating in the district, maybe in the whole chain of over five hundred stores.

I was one of four white women on the staff of about seventy; most of the others were African American, Latina/o, or second-generation Asian American. Almost every worker in the store spoke Black English, including some of my white and Latina/o coworkers. The customers were an amazing mix. I would often marvel at how our "guests" (as we were required to call them) seemed to represent every racial/ethnic group and every social class. Rich ladies with diamond rings shopped next to very poor families who were dirty and shabbily dressed. Recent immigrants from Africa, India, and Central America were also there, some in traditional garb.

The other store where I worked, which I call Diamond Toys, was located in a upscale urban shopping district. Although it was a mere ten miles away from the Toy Warehouse, it was a world apart. Diamond Toys was a popular tourist destination, written up in guidebooks and often featured in the newspaper at Christmastime (during which I worked there). This high-priced store was also part of a national chain and also employed a staff of about seventy. But its racial composition was opposite to that of the Toy Warehouse: only three African Americans worked at the store (all women); the majority of the staff were white. Most of the customers were white too and were either middle or upper class.

The other major distinction between the two stores was that only one of them, Diamond Toys, was unionized. Union membership in the United States is at its lowest point in a hundred years, a reflection not only of the conservative political climate in America at the start of the twenty-first century but also of the interests of the big box retailers, who have unprecedented political and economic power, especially at the local level. Wal-Mart, for example, is notorious for its union-busting activities and violations of local labor laws and zoning ordinances.[6]

What was decidedly not different between the two stores was the merchandise we sold. The same toys were sold at the Toy Warehouse and Diamond Toys, despite the widespread impression among the general public that the toys available at Diamond Toys were superior and not available at the Toy Warehouse. Granted, there were a few "exclusives" sold only in each of these stores, but these made very superficial claims to uniqueness. For example, both stores sold "exclusive" Barbies: the one at the Toy Warehouse was outfitted in a sweatshirt with "Toy Warehouse" written on it, while the one sold at Diamond Toys had a shopping bag with the company logo on it. Similarly, one store featured a giant stuffed panda bear as a mascot, the other, a giant lion. Only the social contexts—and the prices—were different.

Why would someone choose to shop at the more expensive store? From economists' perspective, consumer choice is based on a simple cost-benefit calculation: they assume that we all want the most value for the lowest price. Because consumers are, in their view, rational maximizers of self-interest, the obvious choice for the toy shopper should be the Toy Warehouse, with its easy parking, enormous selection, and low prices (see, for example, Corstjens and Corstjens 1995).[7] Sociologists have spent a great deal of time and effort criticizing the application of this economic, utilitarian model to social behavior in general, but we have apparently conceded its value for understanding economic behavior. There is a good reason for this: the model is very successful at predicting shopping behavior. Most shoppers do pick the Toy Warehouse. The big box superstore has transformed the retail environment. Ritzer (1999) reports that 80 percent of all new retail space in 1994 was occupied by superstores, accounting for one-third of all retail revenue in the United States.

But the choice of where to shop is not always decided by the most convenience and the lowest price. In her book *The Overspent American*, Juliet Schor (1998) analyzes the appeal of high-priced brands and specialty stores. She argues that middle- and upper-middle-class consumers sometimes prefer to shop at expensive stores because doing so marks their social distance from lower-class, and thus presumably less refined, shoppers. This is the case even when the same merchandise is available at Wal-Mart and at an upscale boutique—an increasingly likely possibility due to the subcontracting of production in overseas factories. Rich Americans are willing to pay a premium for goods with a designer label purchased at specialty stores because these items symbolize their owner's superior "taste, individuality, and exclusivity" (147). As I will argue in this book, social hierarchies not only of class but also of gender and race are enacted in consumers' decisions to shop in higher-priced stores.

Focusing on the point of sale ignores the fundamentally social processes involved in consumer behavior, including how the shopping experience is shaped by race, gender, and social class. A growing number of social theorists are urging a rethinking of consumer behavior along these lines. Daniel Miller (1995), for example, encourages sociologists to study the links between consumers and the larger political economy, paying special attention to the roles played by corporations and states in shaping our consumer choices and to the implications of consumer choice for the workers who produce the goods and services.

The stakes are high. Miller argues that consumption is the key to understanding contemporary alienation as well as potential liberation. He argues that, increasingly, we construct our identities and forge relationships through our purchases, not through our productive activity. In contrast to the time when Marx was writing, most Americans now have minimal or tangential relationships to production, but we do spend a lot of time shopping. Miller (1995, 17) writes, "It is not the proletariat today whose transformation of consciousness would liberate the world, but the consumer. Today, consumption is more the problem than the solution. However, this historical moment may provide the foundation for formulating ideas of how societies might develop in the future."

The possibility that making different consumer choices can lead us to a more just society is a theme repeated in a variety of popular media: in books (*Fast Food Nation, The Overspent American*), movies (Michael Moore's docudramas, for instance), and even presidential campaigns (Ralph Nader's is one example). Environmental degradation, rampant exploitation of third-world workers, and public health catastrophes have all been linked to first-world consumer choices (Schlosser 2001; Schor 1998). Changing those choices is seen as key to solving some of the world's most pressing social problems.

This book explores the social construction of shopping and the implications of consumer choice for social inequality. I am especially interested in understanding how shopping in general and toy shopping in particular are implicated in reproducing gender, race, and class inequalities. The two stores I studied offer two different types of shopping experience: Diamond Toys cultivates its image as the purveyor of high-quality toys sold by a knowledgeable sales staff, while the Toy Warehouse's advertising strategy emphasizes its low prices on a vast array of popular toys. In the chapters that follow, I examine how the two stores also differ in their labor policies and practices, social relations between customers and service workers, and the cultural norms of shopping. I argue that neither store represents a "better" choice for society: both reproduce social inequality, but they do so in different ways.

By highlighting the fundamentally social aspects of consumerism, my goal is to expose how it promotes and bolsters social inequality. But this is not a book opposed to consumerism. I do not advocate a return to a romanticized past when people made everything they consumed. Like most middle-class Americans, I have ambivalent feelings about consumerism. For me, shopping can be both a pleasurable distraction and a laborious chore, a means to express my individuality and to forge bonds with others, an activity at once discretionary and mandatory, highly personal and inherently social.

My feelings of ambivalence are mirrored in a debate that is raging between the defenders of consumerism and its detractors. On the one side are those who see consumerism as a pleasurable source of individual choice, a form of playfulness, and even a marker of political freedom. Certainly, marketing professionals, advertisers, and corporate executives fall into this category, but so do a number of postmodernist and feminist theorists. These theorists argue that because objects in material culture have no single set of meanings, producers cannot control how people use their commodities. Far from being duped, consumers exercise agency and creativity in transforming and appropriating the goods they acquire. Their purposes are varied: objects can express whimsical feelings of desire or disgust, or they can be used to make profound political statements that aim to upend the status quo.

Among the first proponents of this perspective was Dick Hebdige (1979), who studied the consumer practices of the punk subculture, which he described as a bricolage of commodities sometimes literally ripped out of their intended setting and subverted to represent antiestablishment views. A more recent example of the willful subversion of commodities was the popularity of upscale Calvin Klein merchandise among the Los Angeles Bloods gang in the 1980s. The insignia "CK" was worn to express the gang's rivalry with the Crips (i.e., Crip Killer). Black Knight athletic gear was worn by the Crips for the same reason (i.e., Blood Killer). Neither Calvin Klein nor Black Knight intended its products to be used for these purposes.

Many feminists are also drawn to this approach with its emphasis on the active, subversive, and resistant consumer. Viewing shoppers this way counters the popular stereotype of women consumers as unthinking, conservative, and readily manipulated by men corporate executives and advertisers. Cultural theorists Janice Radway (1984), Angela McRobbie (1991), and Rana Emerson (2002), for instance, argue that women's consumption of an apparently sexist popular culture can be understood as a critique of patriarchy and even racism. Emerson (2002) argues that when young African American women watch music videos that show images of hypersexual black women, they may fantasize about being sexually powerful yet cherished and appreciated by men. Imagining a better reality is the first step in challenging the status quo.

On the other side of the debate are those who see consumerism as promoting opportunism, insecurity, and disenchantment. Here the dominant voices are from Marxists, globalization critics, and participants in simplicity movements, who view consumerism as inherently opposed to the achievement of fulfilling social relationships and meaningful lives. Our consumer culture is the ultimate outcome of a process of rationalization of society that we are powerless to transform, let alone control. George Ritzer (1999), one of the leading sociological critics of globalization, argues that we are increasingly helpless in the face of mega–shopping centers, which lead and even coerce us into hyperconsumerism. New palaces of consumption draw us in with spectacle and entertainment but then trap us into a cycle of buying that inevitably leads to boredom, dehumanization, and loss of meaningful social relationships (see also Willis 1991).

The only solution to the problem, in this view, is to buy less. Juliet Schor (1998), for example, argues that the cure for the malaise of the affluent consumer is to aspire to a simpler lifestyle in which human relationships are not mediated by high-priced consumer goods. Cecile Andrews (2000, 485) recommends the formation of "simplicity circles," voluntary study groups that encourage members to "turn away from activities like shopping and career climbing, which don't give real satisfaction," and to embrace "creativity, community and the celebration of daily life," which bring "true joy and meaning." Activists have also joined in the chorus: highly publicized international protests against the

World Trade Organization, the World Bank, McDonald's, and Starbucks criticize the affluent Western lifestyle that relies on the continuing exploitation and degradation of poor people around the globe. The recommendation is to avoid buying and "do it yourself" (DIY) by recycling what you have, growing your own food, supporting cooperatives, and buying things only at second-hand stores. This DIY movement, which counts many young people among its advocates, reflects both a political statement against capitalism and a rejection of consumerism as the means to achieve a happy and fulfilled life.

I ally myself with neither side of this debate. I agree that consumption is increasingly the means through which we forge our identities and stake out our political loyalties and commitments. But I also agree that consumerism is controlled by corporations that are not accountable to human needs or to the general good of society. In taking this in-between position, I am joining the ranks of a growing number of scholars who argue that consumerism isn't entirely good or bad (see, for example, Gabriel 2004; Humphery 1998; Miller 1995; Seiter 1993). Just like any social trend, consumerism harms us all in some ways and benefits us in others. Of course, the costs are not borne by everyone equally; nor does everyone partake in the same benefits. The social relations of consumption, like the social relations of production or the social relations of family life, reflect ongoing and dynamic power struggles between different groups (for example, between men and women, bourgeoisie and proletariat, dominant whites and subordinated racial/ethnic minorities). In my view, history and social context are key to understanding the moral value of consumerism at any given time or place.

My goal, then, is not to criticize consumerism but to analyze its current social organization. My specific contribution is to describe how gender, race, and social class shape the retail trade industry. Under altered conditions, I suggest, shopping can contribute to a greater social good. Under current conditions, it makes social inequality worse.

STUDYING SHOPPING

This book is based primarily on observations I made while working at the two toy stores. I chose the method of participant observation instead of interviewing or surveys to enable me to experience firsthand the dynamic interactions of the shopping floor from both sides of the counter. I applied for five jobs over the course of this study and was hired for two. I will speculate on some of the reasons I wasn't hired for the others later in the book. But I think that the main reason I got the jobs I did and not the others had more to do with timing than anything else. For retail work of this type, job applicants have to be in the right place at the right time, available to start work immediately, and with flexible schedules that suit the needs of the stores. In both cases when I was hired, an orientation for new employees had already been planned for the following day, and I could fit in perfectly with the store's training schedule. Had I applied a day later, I believe I would have been out of luck.

A successful applicant must appear unencumbered by other responsibilities. Once I understood this point I decided to tell potential employers that I didn't have another job. This was the only way I misrepresented myself to my employers. I told them that I was a college teacher (from Texas) and that I wanted to learn about retail. I gave as references the chair of my department and one of my colleagues. (Store managers never called them.) I did not tell my employers that I was planning to return to college teaching because they would not have hired me. I also did not seek official approval from management to conduct a formal study with interviews. Workers are often suspicious of researchers who have managerial approval, treating them like corporate spies. Ruth Milkman (1997) discovered this in her study of auto workers. In her candid account, she discusses how the factory workers she studied opened up to her only *after* she abandoned her official credentials, something she initially had struggled hard to obtain. This is not surprising. As organizations seek to cut labor costs, researchers are often brought in to monitor employee productivity and shop-floor culture, and their conclusions usually harm workers. Workers have every reason to fear a management-approved researcher.

My friends and colleagues who knew about my venture into the toy stores were curious about what my coworkers thought of me. Wasn't it obvious that I wasn't really a salesclerk? Didn't my Ph.D. make me stand out? What was it like to be undercover? But the fact is, I was never undercover. When I was working at these stores, I really was a salesclerk. No one knew that I was also a professor (except the personnel managers who hired me), no one asked, and I'm pretty sure that no one cared. My coworkers had their own problems. I quickly learned that it was considered rude to ask about a coworker's background, since it was understood that no one intentionally sought a low-wage retail job. To the question "Why do you work here?" most would answer, "Because they were hiring," or perhaps, "Because IKEA never called back." It is a middle-class conceit to think that where you work is a reflection of your interests, values, and aptitudes. In the world of low-wage retail work, no one assumes that people choose their occupations or that their jobs reflect who they really are.

At Diamond Toys, I was not the only salesclerk with advanced degrees. A number of my coworkers had to take their jobs to tide themselves over through difficult financial times. Carl was a practicing attorney, Dennis was a teacher, Joan was an actor, and a few others had computer degrees, having previously worked for failed dot-com businesses. No one dwelled openly on their unused credentials.

Like all other new hires, I started at the very bottom. I had to obey the orders of my managers and supervisors. I had a variety of supervisors, including a nineteen-year-old Pakistani American man, a twenty-five-year-old white man, and a fifty-five-year-old African American woman. Learning to take orders was the hardest part of the job for me. If I thought a policy was wrong or misguided I had to keep my mouth shut (a habit not nurtured in tenured professors) because no one cared about my opinions. I was reprimanded once for talking back at the Toy Warehouse. Luckily I didn't suffer any demerits because of it, but it almost made me quit my job.

I worked about six weeks at each store. This was long enough to detect patterns in store operations and interactions but not long enough to conduct a proper ethnography. Anthropologists typically stay in the field for at least a year, with the goal of gaining intimate access to the culture and the inner lives of the people in a community. In this study I did not attempt to get inside the minds of the workers or the shoppers or to explore their private lives. Rather I attempted to describe and analyze the rules that govern giant toy stores. My goal was to understand how shopping was socially organized and how it might be transformed to enhance the lives of workers and consumers.

In the next chapter, I examine the history of toy retailing in the United States. This chapter provides important context for understanding the social organization of large retailers like the Toy Warehouse and Diamond Toys. Over the course of the twentieth century, toy stores became bigger, owing to the twin forces of suburbanization and deregulation. The organization of retail work also changed as stores began employing first working-class and later middle-class white women. Jobs were restructured over the course of the century, becoming more "flexible," part time, and temporary to accommodate longer shopping hours and to resist unionization. Finally, toys themselves changed radically, especially in the fifty years leading up to 2005. Direct marketing to children, which began with the Barbie doll in the late 1950s, changed the nature of the toys offered for sale and spurred debates over censoring children's media that continue today.

The subsequent three chapters explore different dimensions of shopping and selling, drawing on my observations at the two stores. In chapter 3, I discuss the social organization of the two stores, including the job hierarchies, working conditions, benefits, and pay. Workers are sorted into jobs on the bases of race and gender, resulting in advantages for white men (and, to a lesser extent, white women) and blocked opportunities for racial/ethnic minority women and men. For most shopping-floor workers, however, retail is hard, grinding labor that pays poorly and offers few benefits or opportunities for advancement. Although, as I will show, a union helps to ameliorate some of the most egregious aspects of the job by guaranteeing hours and providing some benefits, even unionized jobs do not always pay a living wage.

Chapter 4 examines the interactions between clerks and customers. Toy stores today are marketed as themed environments. Corporate boards imagine an ideal customer and an ideal worker, and they establish rules to govern the layout of the store and the comportment of clerks to achieve these imagined ideals. However, as I will show, these rules are often manipulated by both clerks and customers in ways that take into account the shifting mix of class, race, and gender involved in face-to-face transactions. The result is that shopping interactions often reproduce social inequality.

Chapter 5 reports on my observations of adults and children in the toy store. Adults teach children how to shop. These lessons involve both overt instruction on accounting and value and covert lessons about social inequality. Adults' dreams and aspirations for children are also reflected in the toys they buy, which often celebrate and reinscribe stereotypes of race, gender, and social class. Of course, children have their own ideas about toys, with the result that a great deal of conflict takes place within the store.

The final chapter turns to the possibilities for creating a more equitable consumer society. I review a number of consumer and worker movements that are addressing the perils of rampant consumerism, low-wage work, and the racism and sexism embedded in consumer goods and practices. I argue that creating an alliance of workers and consumers that can address their mutual economic and moral concerns will be key to transforming the shopping experience to make it more equitable and socially responsible.

Like my predecessor, Annie Marion MacLean, I believe that

the public has a duty to demand and uphold the dignity of low-wage retail workers. I agree with her that consumers should ponder the economic and social consequences of their shopping choices and that they should refuse to shop in stores "where evils exist." But, also like MacLean, I believe that new legislation and enforcement of existing labor laws are needed to transform this industry. A rekindled commitment to our responsibilities as citizen consumers is ultimately required to rid shopping of its attendant evils.

HISTORY OF TOY SHOPPING IN AMERICA

I don't remember ever going to a toy store as a child. Although specialty toy stores existed in major cities like New York and Chicago as early as the 1860s, in the towns and suburbs where I lived no store had the primary purpose of selling toys to kids.[1] I remember hobby stores that sold electric train sets and model-building kits, sporting goods stores where you could buy bikes and baseballs, and department stores and dime stores that had toy departments, but these stores sold merchandise primarily to adults, not to children.

Something radical happened in the intervening thirty-plus years in the marketing and selling of toys. Giant toy stores now dot the landscape, offering huge selections and low prices on toys made all over the world. This chapter is devoted to understanding this transformation. Toy retailing has undergone three significant changes in its social organization over the past century. First, the size, economic power, and location of stores have changed. Retail stores have become bigger, more powerful than manufacturers, and more spread out over suburban and quasi-rural areas. Second, the labor force inside retail stores has undergone profound rearrangement. Retail work that was previously considered appropriate for white family men has become feminized, racially mixed, part time, and temporary. And third, the toys offered for sale inside stores have changed. In contrast to a generation ago, virtually every toy brought to market today has television and movie tie-ins. Exploring the history of toy stores can give clues to where the retail industry is headed and how that future course might be altered.

DEVELOPMENT OF RETAIL GIANTS

Where we shop has changed dramatically over the last century. Prior to the 1950s, the major centers of retail trade were in cities. Those living in suburban or rural settings relied on small local stores, catalog sales, or dime store chains to purchase goods. From the late 1950s through the 1970s, suburban shopping malls were developed on the outskirts of cities on unincorporated land. These original shopping malls were modeled on community-centered downtowns, albeit stripped of their unruly and unsanitary elements. Lizabeth Cohen (1998, 199) writes that the early mall developers took steps to eliminate not only vagrants and prostitutes but also racial minorities and poor people from the shopping landscape. These original shopping malls declined in the 1980s, when they were replaced by big box stores, so called because they are shaped like warehouses, have no windows, and are fronted by large parking lots. Big box stores teamed up in new developments called "power centers" on undeveloped land located near highways on the edges of suburbs (Ortega 1998, 294). Factory outlet malls are another recent trend in retail development: these large groupings of stores, originally located in rural areas, sell discounted factory-direct name-brand merchandise.

This trend may have already peaked. In 1996, there were 329 centers in the United States, but by 2003 their number had dwindled to 230 (Pristin 2004).

The original movement of retail stores, from urban center to suburban shopping mall, was overdetermined by a number of social and political changes after World War II. Stores followed the general out-migration of the middle class from cities, brought about by mortgage lending practices that favored suburban development. Suburbs were based on a gender division of labor in the family in which women were assigned primary domestic responsibilities (including shopping) and men were expected to be the family breadwinners. Although shopping for the family has always been considered "women's work," the suburban migration cemented that link by geographically segregating consumerism from the "productive" activity of men: Women now shopped in the suburbs where they lived instead of traveling to cities, where men commuted to work every day. "White flight" was also a factor in this suburbanization of the population, as many whites moved to residentially segregated suburban neighborhoods in response to new civil rights laws that mandated the racial integration of schools. The suburbanization of shopping was also made possible by the ubiquitous spread of private automobiles and government-subsidized highways. In her book *A Consumers' Republic*, Lizabeth Cohen (2003, 266) emphasizes that the first suburban shopping malls were built with the assumption that customers would be white, middle-class women who had cars.

Another significant cause for the movement of retail out of urban centers was a 1954 change in tax laws. Thomas Hanchett (1996) demonstrates that new "accelerated depreciation" allowances in the 1950s underwrote the original suburban mall developments. This tax policy permitted developers to write off the costs of new business buildings and claim losses against unrelated income. Although it was originally intended to spur the construction of rental housing, investors instead used this tax law to turn the construction of suburban shopping centers into lucrative tax shelters in the late 1950s and 1960s. Basically, the law allowed developers to deduct the full amount of depreciation on their new construction within the first few years of the project's life instead of gradually deducting the replacement value over the expected thirty- to forty-year life span of the structure. This meant that shopping mall owners could deduct a large percentage of their investments in the first years of business, enabling them to earn quick and hefty profits even if the retail stores in the mall were not making money. Importantly, these financial returns could be made only on new construction; renovation of existing businesses was not favored by accelerated depreciation, so downtown shopping centers were unable to reap any benefit from the tax law. Accelerated depreciation led to a suburban retail building frenzy, so that by 1971, according to Hanchett (1996, 1108), there were close to seven shopping centers for every 100,000 Americans (compared to 0.95 centers for every 100,000 in 1956). Paradoxically, the accelerated depreciation allowances were rarely used to maintain the new structures because owners were not obligated to actually use the money to pay for replacement costs as the buildings became dilapidated. Thus, by 1970, entire shopping centers were in decline while construction of new, larger centers continued nearby (Hanchett 1996, 1103).

Giant retail stores can no longer rely on such lucrative tax shelters to finance new developments. In 1986, Congress revised the depreciation allowance because of worries about severe overbuilding. But stores like Wal-Mart no longer need a mortgage to set up a new outlet; they can buy the land and finance the building construction themselves (Ortega 1998, 294). Yet public financing continues to play a role in underwriting new stores. A number of towns and cities now offer tax breaks for new retail developments, hoping that the sales tax revenues generated by new "power malls" and factory outlet malls will shore up declining revenues received from state and federal governments. Municipalities compete with each other to offer shopping center developers ever-larger tax incentives, which ironically have been shown to offset any advantages that come from increased sales tax revenue. In an even more unfortunate irony, cities and towns that have successfully organized to prevent the building of new suburban retail malls (in order to protect their local downtowns) find that the big box stores can easily subvert these goals by locating right across the city line. This means that the neighboring community will reap whatever tax benefit the new store generates and the downtown merchants located in the protesting town will suffer anyway as many of their customers begin to patronize the giant discounters (Nordquist 2003).

How did retailers become so big, rich, and powerful? In the first half of the twentieth century, retail stores were relatively powerless compared to the manufacturers. Manufacturers produced the name-brand items that stores wanted to stock and had the power to set prices for their goods. But in the second half of the twentieth century, the relative power of retailers and manufacturers flipped. Today, the retail giants determine what they will offer for sale in their stores and how much they will charge for the merchandise. Their high-volume buying power can make or break a manufacturer. They can and do demand low pricing, and if producers are unable to meet those requirements, the retailers move to another supplier or open their own factories overseas (Frank 1999).[2]

This change in the relationship between retailers and manufacturers was partly a result of the federal government's deregulation of trade. In 1978, the Federal Trade Commission (FTC) outlawed the practice of manufacturers' setting the price for their goods. Price fixing was never the law of the land (it was contrary to the Sherman Anti-Trust Act guaranteeing free trade), but from the Great Depression through the 1970s several states authorized the practice as a way to ensure "fair trade." Also known as "retail price maintenance," fair trade laws (as they were known by their advocates) gave manufacturers the right to set prices for their goods as an expression of their patent rights and copyrights. This meant that all stores that carried "brand-name" merchandise had to agree to sell it at the same, agreed-upon price. Small retailers were often seen as the beneficiaries of these laws because, unlike large department stores, they could not offer discounts on popular items and afford to stay in business (Bluestone et al. 1981; Hollander 1986 [1954]).

Large department stores, like Macy's, fought price restrictions, and many stores found ways to subvert the regulations. Macy's department store began in the nineteenth century as a discounter promising the lowest prices on popular goods (Hower 1943). It undercut competitors all the time, which it could do because of its "cash down" policy (that is, no credit was offered). After 1900, Macy's came under increasing attack for its price cutting, seen at the time as an unethical business practice. Between 1900 and 1914, Macy's was involved in a number of lawsuits by manufac-

turers charging that the store violated their patent rights by selling their goods at a lower-than-agreed-upon price. Although
Macy's won most of these battles (including one that made it to
the Supreme Court in 1913), fair trade legislation passed in subsequent decades restricted its ability to offer discounts on popular brands.[3]

It is hard to imagine from our vantage point today, but for
most of the twentieth century, the very idea of discounting was
considered unseemly. An economist writing at midcentury noted
that many business professors and textbook writers of the time
did not discuss discounting because it was considered in some
trade circles to be "unethical" and not quite "respectable" (Hollander 1986 [1954], 14). Newspapers often refused to accept advertisements from discount stores (Brecher 1949a). Even consumers were wary of the practice. A 1949 article in *Consumer
Reports* entitled "Buying at a Discount: Is It against the Law?"
(Brecher 1949a) summed up the concern. The article emphasized
that consumers needn't worry about buying goods at discount.
The enforcement of fair trade laws was a private matter between
manufacturers and retailers and as such had unpredictable results
even for defendants in civil court cases. Consumers could never
face criminal charges of discount shopping. Nevertheless, *Consumer Reports* stopped short of fully endorsing discount shopping,
sending a very mixed message to consumers. Earlier in the same
year, the organization sent undercover shoppers to investigate
discount stores in cities around the country. This research found
over one hundred "admitted" discount houses in New York City,
twelve in Chicago, eight in Los Angeles, five in Seattle, and two
in Baltimore. The magazine concluded that "buying at a discount

is a widespread practice" but refused to disclose the names of the discount stores in order to protect them from potential damage suits. To consumers interested in bargain shopping, it offered the following advice on "how to find a discount house": "If you want to find a discount house in your own city, don't write to CU [Consumer Union, publisher of *Consumer Reports*]. Instead, ask your friends and acquaintances, the man in your company who does the company's purchasing, people you know who are in the retail business, or others in a position to know. By all odds the most effective way to find a discount house is to ask other people" (Brecher 1949b, 375). Not surprisingly, the general impression of consumers was that buying goods at discounts was something done under the table; it was certainly not an aspect of shopping to brag about.

That all changed when the FTC ended retail price fixing in 1978, a time when economic liberalization was sweeping through government. Not only retail but also the airline industry was deregulated. (Prior to the 1970s the government had approved airline routes and fares.) The FTC deregulation of retail meant that products could have a "suggested retail price" from the manufacturer but not a mandatory price.

The impact on manufacturer-retail relationships was immediate and profound. Prior to deregulation, most retail stores controlled the merchandising and display of commodities but not their design or manufacture. The two were part of a team, with retailers reliant on trademarked brands advertised by manufacturers to lure customers into their stores and manufacturers reliant on retailers to sell their goods at a minimum price to maintain their profits. But once the FTC undercut the manufacturer's retail price, the manufacturer and retailer became competing companies. In his history of the Gap stores, Louis Nevaer (2001) points out that after 1978 the manufacturer and retailer were no longer *allowed* to cooperate with each other on price fixing because that would now be defined as collusion, an illegal business practice.

This story of deregulation is important for understanding the rise of large discount toy chains in the 1970s and 1980s. The demise of manufacturer price fixing inspired increased competition among retailers to offer discounted goods. Stores were forced to cut their profit margins on the sale of name-brand goods and increase their size in the hope that a high volume of trade would keep them afloat. Giant toy stores like the Toy Warehouse where I worked are called "category killers" by marketing experts.[4] This term is used when the discounter strategy is applied to one category of merchandise, like food, pet care, or toys. The discounter strategy is "developing large sites and maximizing efficiency, building high volume with low prices, and then negotiating appropriate discounts from manufacturers, investing in technology and reducing logistics costs" (Corstjens and Corstjens 1995, 101). The goal of the category killers is to control the entire market for the goods they sell. If successful, they can demand concessions from manufacturers, who must give giant stores incentives to place their products on the shelves.

The "golden age" of the category killer was the 1990s (Corstjens and Corstjens 1995, 103). Since then, the category killers have come under siege by giant discounters like Wal-Mart and Target, which can offer even lower prices because they can sell more merchandise due to their higher volume of trade. The

Toy Warehouse is now struggling to keep up with Wal-Mart, now the largest toy retailer, indeed the largest private employer, in the country (Michman and Mazze 2001).

Under these circumstances of competitive discount pricing, according to Nevaer, the only way for retailers to ensure profitability is to manufacture their own brands. Profits still can be made at the manufacturing stage by sending production overseas to factories employing workers at extremely low wages. The Gap was the first store to pursue this strategy of "vertical integration," an approach that was quickly replicated by other retailers. When the Gap first opened in 1969, 90 percent of the clothes it sold were manufactured by Levi's in factories located throughout the United States. At that time, Levi's controlled the price of its clothing, so the price charged by the Gap was pretty much the same as that of any other place. After deregulation, the percentage of Levi's sold in Gap stores steadily declined, and Levi's were replaced by Gap jeans. By 1991, all of the clothes sold in the Gap were manufactured by the Gap in overseas factories.

Giant toy stores are not vertically integrated in this way, since they do not make their own toys, but they do make deals with manufacturers to produce store "exclusives"—that is, toys specially made for sale only in their stores. Thus Mattel makes a special Barbie doll available only at the Toy Warehouse and another available only at Diamond Toys. But stores are not allowed to control the distribution of manufacturers' products. In 1997, the FTC won its case against the toy store giant Toys "R" Us, which was charged with illegally pressuring toy makers into not selling popular toys to warehouse clubs, a ruling that the store immediately appealed (Miller 1998). Any collusion between stores and manufacturers is dubious from a legal perspective unless the store owns—or directly subcontracts from—the manufacturer.

Since they do not manufacture their own products, toy stores attempt to develop brand loyalty to the stores themselves. The shopping experience itself is now sold to consumers. Retailers want customers to think of their stores as a destination, not a mere outlet for the distribution of products. Their goal is to move attention away from the products sold, which are available anywhere, even over the Internet, to the place where the products are sold. Thus toy stores today have become brands marketed directly to children (more about that later). "I'm a Toys 'R' Us kid," says one jingle featured on TV advertisements. What the kid is buying is irrelevant; where the kid shops matters more. With this strategy, retailers win and manufacturers lose.

There are stores that opt out of the discounter wars. Diamond Toys is an example, and so are the scattered specialty toy shops often located in neighborhood shopping districts. These stores emphasize status, the reputedly high quality and/or unique merchandise they sell, and excellent service. The goal of Diamond Toys is to attract a wealthy, cosmopolitan clientele seeking unique, high-quality toys sold by solicitous, knowledgeable service workers (although, as I will point out in a later chapter, this describes the store's image more than its reality). Stores in the Diamond Toys chain are generally located in upscale shopping districts in major cities and are built to resemble amusement parks, making them appeal to tourists as well as to the wealthy. Other specialty retailers (such as Zany Brainy) focus their inventory on educational, nonviolent, and nonsexist toys. These stores hire former educators and learning specialists to assist adults in making their toy selections. Altogether, these specialty toy stores command less than 10 percent of the total toy market. The number of these niche stores has dwindled over time as the stores have become increasingly unable to compete with the category killers and giant discounters (Michman and Mazze 2001).

LABOR HISTORY

Not only the stores but also the people who work inside stores have changed over the past hundred years. In the early decades of the twentieth century, a typical retail worker was a native-born Anglo-Saxon man who was educated, knowledgeable about the specific merchandise he sold, married, and earning salary plus commission. A 1925 photograph taken inside the first Sears store in Chicago shows an all-male staff serving an all-female clientele (Worthy 1984). By the middle of the century, the typical employee had changed: the salesclerk was more likely to be a woman of any race, very young or very old, earning low wages on a part-time or temporary basis, with little or no prior experience (Glazer 1993, 68).

According to Nona Glazer, women made their first inroads into retail when stores transitioned from clerk service to self-service, a process that happened gradually between 1910 and 1960. This transition went along with the standardization of measures and the rise of national advertising. The idea behind self-serve was to replace the expertise of the clerk with the expertise of the customer: instead of relying on the worker for information about the products sold, the customer entered the store with knowledge acquired from advertising campaigns. Packaging was part of this transformation: an increasing number of goods were purchased in factory-sealed containers. This standardization was brought about in part through demands by consumer groups as a hedge against fraud and adulterated contents. Consumers increasingly relied on information printed on the packages to make their selections instead of consulting with salesclerks.

There were exceptions to this general trend. Dime stores relied on an exclusively female sales force from their inception in the 1880s (Raucher 1991). Some department stores were also an early exception to this gendered pattern of retail service work. Women were the preferred clerks at Macy's, where they composed up to 90 percent of the workforce in the 1870s (Hower 1943). According to Susan Porter Benson (1986), managers attempted to "match" the characteristics of department store salesclerks to the characteristics of shoppers, which meant that most saleswomen were native-born whites. Age was important, as clerks increasingly were expected to model the merchandise they sold (small discounts on merchandise sometimes were allowed for this reason). Men weren't suitable as department store salesclerks, it was thought, because they could be flirtatious and not adequately solicitous.[5]

However, virtually all store managers were men. Variety chain stores like Woolworth, JC Penney, and W. T. Grant sought "average country boys" to run their stores, putting a premium on hiring men who matched the racial/ethnic backgrounds of the rural communities where they were first located. These men were expected to be upstanding members of the community, to "wear jackets and not to wear hats or to smoke" (Raucher 1991, 138). According to Raucher, Woolworth sought clean-cut, honest managers in order to "assure mothers that they could entrust their daughters to a company that protected its salesgirls from any 'insult.' Company policy required the dismissal of any man, regardless of his record otherwise, caught making sexual advances to female employees or drinking in public" (141).

While dime stores preferred to hire young women, usually teenagers living at home, department stores like Macy's would have preferred to hire middle-class women to be salesclerks. But because these women had higher-paying alternative careers, department store managers settled for working-class women. They did endeavor to transform these women into "genteel but deferential workers" (Benson 1986, 5). The goal was to produce an upscale domestic servant who was knowledgeable about the tastes and manners of the bourgeoisie but who would not have the temerity to imitate this upper-class behavior, only to cater to it. Thus workers were trained "to adopt the veneer of a higher class without receiving any of its rights or privileges" (5).

African American women and members of new immigrant groups were not hired as department store clerks, although after World War II black women were sometimes hired as elevator operators and backroom workers (Benson 1986, 209). Early department store policies often barred members of these groups as *customers*, let alone as employees. Stores that would allow black customers would often forbid them from trying on clothes (Cohen 2003, 90). In a notorious example of this racial exclusion, many dime stores in the South allowed African Americans to shop in their stores but not to eat at their lunch counters.

Prior to the dismantling of Jim Crow laws, members of the African American community engaged in a great deal of activism to open consumer access. In the 1930s, for example, several leaders of the black community, including W. E. B. Du Bois, Booker T. Washington, and Marcus Garvey, promoted consumer campaigns to challenge discriminatory hiring practices in stores. They lobbied for public support under the slogan "Don't Buy Where You Can't Work" and advocated voluntary shopping segregation to support black-owned businesses (Cohen 2003; Weems 1998). African American women organized themselves into "housewives' leagues" in many northern cities to encourage blacks to "support black businesses, buy black-produced products, and patronize black professionals" (Weems 1998, 58). Consumer boycotts and sit-ins begun in the late 1950s successfully publicized and challenged the exclusionary rules in many stores. Although these strategies galvanized national support for integration, whites sometimes retaliated by boycotting stores that treated blacks as equals (Weems 1998, 65).

The 1964 passage of the Civil Rights Act brought an end to the legality of racist shopping restrictions. But by then the suburbanization of retail and the decline of urban centers were well underway, spurred along by "white flight" protesting the new integration laws. So while the most egregious symbols of racism were removed from stores after 1964—"whites only" rest rooms and drinking fountains were eliminated—the law did little to enhance African Americans' job opportunities in the retail industry. Indeed, as Weems (1998) argues, improved access to previously whites-only stores undermined support for many black-owned businesses, which often lacked the capital to compete for consumer dollars. In his view, "white owned businesses, rather than unfettered black consumers, were the primary beneficiaries of the Civil Rights Act of 1964" (69).

White married women were the preferred employees in the first suburban shopping centers that opened in the 1960s. Their jobs were designed as temporary and part time and were advertised as a means to acquire new friendships, not financial independence (Cohen 2003). Cohen argues that this labor strategy was purposely intended to break union control of retail stores, and it worked. Women shopping mall clerks earned minimum wages without benefits.[6]

By then, however, white women had made inroads into retail management. A 1949 survey reported in the *Journal of Retailing* heralded a "feminine invasion of executive positions" in department and specialty stores (Gerstenberg and Ellsworth 1949, 97). A gendered logic justified women's inroads into these previously all-male careers. The survey found that women were the vast majority of fashion coordinators, a position that purportedly drew on their "instinctive color sense, plus a feeling for fashion and style" (99). Women composed about half of all auditors, buyers, and personnel directors at the time of the survey, but this too had a "logical" (that is, gendered) explanation, according to the authors: "The intuitive ability of women to understand others combined with a natural patience are characteristics that are highly essential to the effective performance of many of the activities associated with these positions" (101). Thus, over the course of the century, many of the jobs that had previously been seen as demanding "competent, trustworthy, and loyal men" (Raucher 1991, 131) were redefined as appropriate for "intuitive" and "patient" women endowed with "instinctive color sense."

Today retail sales is one of the most diverse sectors of the labor force. But as chapter 3 will discuss, workers are segregated by type of store and stratified hierarchically within stores. In general, the more upscale the store and high paying the position, the more likely the employee will be a white, middle-class woman or man. Discount stores attract a "less refined" sales force, in part because wages are so low and also because the clerk is less involved in the actual work of selling the merchandise to customers. Expensive stores often tout the expertise of their sales staff in their advertising. Customers are urged to believe that spending more at their store for the same products available at the discounters is worth it because the store offers consultation with a professional and knowledgeable salesclerk. Although, as I will argue, these claims to expertise are highly dubious, by hiring workers with race, class, and gender privilege (if they can afford it) these stores signal their commitment to high-quality customer service. Consequently, for those consumers today who have a choice of where to shop, the decision usually involves picking the race, class, and gender of the person who will be serving them.[7]

THE ADVERTISING INDUSTRY AND THE MARKETING OF TOYS

A third major change in the history of toy stores concerns the making and marketing of toys. Toys change radically from one generation, even from one season, to the next. This is a source of dismay to many adults, who tend to see moral decline in the consumer preferences of youth. The toys that delight children today are tacky and incite antisocial urges, in contrast to the wonderful toys of their youth that encouraged imaginative play and meaningful attachments. As Heather Hendershot (1998, 134) observes, "[A]dults of any generation will argue that the products of their own youth were good, whereas today's stuff is bad."

Although the tendency of adults to condemn children's preferences is not new, changes in the advertising and marketing of toys to children have played an important role in shaping the toy preferences of children today. In his history of the toy industry,

Stephen Kline (1993) analyzes the changes in the characteristics of toys that were brought about by the deregulation of TV advertising in the 1980s. Prior to that time, limitations were placed on advertisers who marketed to children. Special care had to be taken when describing the advertised products so as not to confuse fact and fantasy in the minds of kids. Also, the number of minutes of ads shown during children's viewing hours had to be limited. In the 1980s the Federal Communication Commission (FCC) deregulated advertising and did away with most restrictions on TV advertising to kids. The immediate impact, according to Kline, was to open the door to "character marketing"—the use of fictional (animated) cartoon characters to promote products, including toys made in their image. As a direct consequence of this deregulation, most toys sold in America today are character toys. (This is not true in nations with regulated TV marketing, like Sweden, Norway, and England. However, syndication and the availability of cable TV are encroaching on these countries' abilities to regulate children's commercial culture.)

For example, prior to deregulation in the United States, Mattel was prevented from launching a kids' show that featured its popular Hot Wheels toy cars. The very first toy/television program character to benefit from deregulation was "Strawberry Shortcake," which was introduced in the 1980s. By the 1990s, no kids' show was brought to TV without at least one product license associated with it. The economic payoff for toy manufacturers was enormous: the U.S. toy market went from a $2 billion industry in the mid-1970s to over $12 billion in 1986 (Kline 1993, 140). Marketing to children became increasingly sophisticated as toy companies used cutting-edge social science research methods to study children's toy preferences. Research confirmed the power of ads in shaping those preferences and also in enhancing children's negotiating power with their parents. As Kline (1993) observes, advertisers saw themselves as "empowering" children vis-à-vis their parents, but of course they were empowering them only as consumers, not in other ways.

One of the reasons given for the FCC deregulation was the failure of media research to document "harm" to children from viewing and consuming certain media products. Kline (1993) notes that researchers and children's advocates were unable to demonstrate scientific "effects" of the kind now required for regulation. There was growing recognition among media researchers that TV culture isn't like a hypodermic needle that doses viewers with specific desires and needs, duping them into buying the advertisers' products. Instead, the effects of TV watching were recognized as dependent on social, cultural, and psychological context. This more sophisticated understanding of media consumption (often the perspective advocated by postmodernist theorists) ironically resulted in freer rein for marketers to do whatever they wanted to sell products to children (Cook 2000).

Kline (1993) argues that this deregulation fundamentally altered the relationship between children and their toys. He maintains that commercial TV is now the most powerful influence shaping children's choice of toys. This is perhaps not surprising given that children now spend one-third of their waking hours in front of the television. The vast majority of teens have TVs in their bedrooms, as do 26 percent of children under age two (Linn 2004, 5). The power and influence of the commercial media on children are unprecedented (Schor 2004).

The importance of advertising in shaping children's culture is evident on the shelves of toy stores. Kline (1993) points out that there is intense competition for shelf space in toy stores and that retailers today have to be convinced of the prospect of high sales before they commit to a display. This is achieved only through multimedia tie-ins, so the result is a flood of character toys. Thus most children's products now have "personalities" associated with them. If you don't watch children's television or movies, you would be lost in the contemporary toy store. Stores are organized by product lines: Sesame Street, Madeline, Tommy the Train, Spongebob Squarepants, Shrek, and Harry Potter are just a few examples. When I was working in the toy stores, each of these characters had its own display area offering a wide variety of products, including stuffed dolls, talking figurines, backpacks, books, videos, train sets, candies, and board games. The possibilities are endless. I had to start watching Saturday morning cartoons to make sense of it all. Diamond Toys made the practice mandatory: the television in the break room was always supposed to be tuned to Nickelodeon, the cable cartoon network, so that employees could be up to speed on the "hot" character lines in children's merchandise. Because the shelf life of characters is limited—no more than three to six months (Seiter 1993, 199)—constant exposure to television is necessary to stay abreast of the trends.

Kline (1993) maintains that these character toys encourage passivity in children. Toys sold to children today come with "prepackaged" scripts; children's fantasies are governed by the programmed logic of the television shows they consume. This is especially the case with girls' toys, as evidenced by their advertisements: they sparkle and move, and the girl stands back and admires them. Ads for boys' toys, in contrast, often represent the child as part of the action. Thus the boy becomes the Power Ranger while the girl admires Barbie.

Unfortunately, relatively little research documents children's actual use of toys. While it does appear that Kline (1993) is correct in his observations of how toys are advertised and marketed, it is less clear that children use the toys in the ways these images suggest. As Hendershot (1998, 124) argues, "[T]here is no 1-to-1 correspondence between consumption and use of a specific object and its meaning and significance for the child."

However, concerns about the power of advertisers in shaping children's preferences have inspired a number of parent-led campaigns to censor children's television. The history of these efforts is documented by Hendershot (1998) in her book about television regulation before the V-chip. Hendershot, who is mostly critical of these efforts, argues that children's voices are typically missing from adult discussion of what is good or bad for children. The debate plays out between the adults who design and produce movies and television shows for children on one side and parents on the other side. These two groups have different criteria for judging the value of children's programming. Producers decide if a show is successful on the basis of the profitability of the toys and the other products marketed on it. If sex and violence "sell" to children, producers design their programs and products accordingly. Thus they see themselves as catering to already existing demand. In contrast, many parents decide on the value of children's programming on the basis of their beliefs about childhood innocence and vulnerability. According to Hendershot, they seek to protect children from "adult secrets about life, death, sex, and violence" (8). It upsets them when these themes feature prominently in the media that are directed at children, so many have engaged in collective efforts to censor children's programming.

According to Karen Sternheimer (2003), television and other mass media are unfairly blamed for corrupting children. She argues that parents who embrace the idea of childhood innocence must find something to blame for children's misdeeds and that television is a handy scapegoat because it is so ubiquitous. It is something children like that their parents generally don't like (since it is geared to kid-level sensibilities and often challenges adult authority). Moreover, the programs and products advertised are not especially sensitive to class distinctions. Children of all backgrounds watch TV, which may add to the middle-class parent's perception of children's programs as unrefined and possibly corrupting influences.[8]

Another strand of the critique of children's media emanates from the community of child psychologists, which has been waging a campaign to ban all marketing to children. Psychologist Susan Linn (2004), for example, argues that children lack the cognitive abilities and solidified values to defend themselves against marketing tactics that try to sell them products that are dangerous (alcohol, tobacco), antisocial (violent video games, sexy dolls), or unhealthful (fast food and soda). She writes: "Children's capacities—to reason, to see beyond their own needs, and to manage their emotions—develop over time. Their values and behavior are influenced by their experience. Preschoolers are more susceptible to influence than older children and adults. Teenagers can reason more effectively than eight-year-olds, but in addition to being buffeted by storms of hormonal changes, the frontal cortex, which governs higher cognitive functioning, including judgment, is not fully developed until their late teens or early twenties" (183).

According to Linn, marketers seeking "cradle-to-grave" brand loyalty are exploiting this vulnerability of children. Increasingly they are aided by developmental psychologists, who help companies market to children using cutting-edge research and theory. Outraged by the unethical implications of using their science to promote harm to children, a number of psychologists in 1992 demanded that the American Psychological Association (APA) take a stand on the issue. The APA Code of Ethics clearly stated that psychologists had the responsibility to use their knowledge to "contribute to human welfare"; marketing to children does the opposite, they claimed. In response, according to Linn, the APA *eliminated* this statement from its code of ethics in 2003.

Linn looks overseas for examples of governments that have banned advertising to children. The Scandinavian countries ban marketing to children under twelve; New Zealand bans junk food advertising to kids. Linn's goal is to ban advertising to everyone under sixteen.

It is not surprising that some adults turn to censorship, thinking that it is in the best interests of children to protect them from the excesses of consumer capitalism. Many parents feel helpless confronted with children who make incessant demands for toys that they see advertised on TV, and they are repelled by the profit-seeking motives of capitalists who manufacture and sell toys to their children. The danger with the censorship strategy, however, is that it establishes a double standard in the consumer cultures of children and adults. Ironically, the values that are embedded and reproduced in marketing tie-ins for children are similar to those of the consumer landscape confronting adults.

Few researchers acknowledge the double standard in the public's assessment of children's and adults' cultures. Hendershot (1998, 101) wryly points out that adults who consume kid culture are "collectors," while children are considered "slavish dupes." Similarly, Ellen Seiter (1993, 38) notes that adults often see kids' consumer desires as greedy and hedonistic, while failing to recognize similar desires in themselves. She writes, "[P]arents are baffled or revolted by their children's taste for mass market goods, while they fail to recognize their own use of consumption for status purposes." Thus, insofar as children's media culture inculcates questionable values and behavior, it can be seen as imitating adult media culture. Children may want Dora the Explorer and Big Bird, but adults want DKNY and Kenneth Cole. The distinction, if there is one, is hardly profound.

Instead of denying children the pleasures of consumerism through censorship, a more promising approach to addressing these problems is to rethink the role of marketing in creating desires in all of us. Perhaps greater attention should be paid to altering marketing practices to promote health and social responsibility instead of hedonism and status attainment. A number of federal health campaigns (such as antismoking and antidrug campaigns) and social movement organizations (ACT UP, Guerrilla Girls, Adbusters) exemplify this approach, using sophisticated design and high production values in their advertisements to promote the social good. Granted, these campaigns mostly endorse *anti*consumerist agendas, but their examples show that advertisements do not have to be damaging to health and well-being.

These public service ads do recognize that different approaches to marketing to children and adults are warranted. The tactics, images, and story lines that are designed to appeal to adults will not necessarily appeal to children, and vice versa. But what shouldn't vary are the values underlying advertisements and the programs they support. If the goal is to change marketing practices to reflect positive social values, then that change should be reflected in all forms of mass media, not only in those directed to children.

CONCLUSION

Because marketing practices are an integral part of the retail industry, transforming those practices is key to making shopping more responsive to our collective well-being. As this chapter has shown, retail stores have evolved radically over a relatively brief span of time. The size of stores has increased as many have pursued the category-killer or discounter strategies, an innovation made possible by trade liberalization and suburbanization in the 1970s. The composition of the labor force within stores has changed, becoming more female and racially diverse as the jobs have declined in hours, pay, and benefits. And toys themselves have changed, partly in response to media deregulation and partly in response to the increasing role of advertising in shaping children's desires. Not all of these changes serve the best interests of consumers or workers. The rest of this book is devoted to exploring the current social organization of the retail toy industry. This investigation will reveal other aspects of shopping in need of transformation.

THE SOCIAL ORGANIZATION OF TOY STORES

Living in a consumer society means that we come into contact with retail workers almost every day. Over 22.5 million people work in this job, composing the largest sector of the service economy (Sandikci and Holt 1998, 305; U.S. Bureau of Labor Statistics 2004). But unless you have "worked retail," you probably know little about the working conditions of the job. At best, retail workers are taken for granted by consumers, noticed only when they aren't doing their job. At worst, they are stereotyped as either dim-witted or haughty, which is how they are often portrayed on television and in the movies.

Retail jobs, like other jobs in the service sector, have grown in number and changed dramatically over the past decades. Service jobs gradually have replaced manufacturing jobs as part of the general deindustrialization of the U.S. economy. This economic restructuring has resulted in boom times for wealthy American consumers as the prices for many commodities have dropped (a consequence of the movement of production overseas). It has also resulted in an erosion of working conditions for Americans in the bottom half of the economy, including service workers. Retail jobs have become increasingly "flexible," temporary, and part time. Over the past decades, workers in these jobs have experienced a loss of job security and benefits, a diminishment in the power of unions, and a lessening of the value of the minimum wage (McCall 2001). Yet while most retail workers have lost ground, the giant corporations they work for have enjoyed unprecedented prosperity and political clout.

George Ritzer (2002) aptly uses the term *McJobs* to describe the working conditions found in a variety of service industries today. The word is a pun on McDonald's, the fast-food giant that introduced and popularized this labor system. McJobs are not careers; they are designed to discourage long-term commitment. They have short promotion ladders, they provide few opportunities for advancement or increased earnings, and the technical skills they require are not transferable outside the immediate work environment. They target sectors of the labor force that presumably don't "need" money to support themselves or their families: young people looking for "fun jobs" before college; mothers seeking part-time opportunities to fit around their family responsibilities; older, retired people looking for the chance to get out of the house and to socialize.[1] However, this image does not resonate with the increasing numbers of workers in these jobs who are struggling to support themselves and their families (Ehrenreich 2001; Talwar 2002). The marketing of McJobs on television commercials for Wal-Mart and fast-food restaurants obscures the harsh working conditions and low pay that contribute to the impoverished state of the working poor.

In addition to contributing to economic inequality, jobs in the retail industry are structured in ways that enhance inequality by gender and race. Although all retail workers are low paid, white men employed in this industry earn more money than any other group.[2] Overall, about as many men as women work in retail trades, but they are concentrated in different kinds of stores. For example, men make up more than three quarters of workers in retail jobs selling motor vehicles, lumber, and home and auto supplies, while women predominate in apparel, gift, and needlework stores (U.S. Bureau of Labor Statistics 2004).

In both stores where I worked, the gender ratio was about 60:40, with women outnumbering men. I was surprised that so many men worked in these toy stores. In my admittedly limited experience, I associated women with the job of selling toys. But I learned that because of the way that jobs are divided and organized, customers usually don't see the substantial numbers of men who are working there too.

Retail work is also organized by race and ethnicity. Ten percent of all employees in the retail trade industry are African American, and 12 percent are of Hispanic origin, slightly less then their overall representation in the U.S. population. But again, whites, African Americans, and Latinas/os are likely to work in different types of stores. For example, African Americans are underrepresented (less than 5 percent) in stores that sell hardware, gardening equipment, and needlework supplies and overrepresented (more than 15 percent) in department stores, variety stores, and shoe stores. Similarly Latina/os are underrepresented (less than 6 percent) in bookstores and gas stations and overrepresented (more than 16 percent) in retail florists and household appliance stores (U.S. Bureau of Labor Statistics 2004).[3]

The two stores where I worked had radically different racial compositions. Sixty percent of the workers at the Toy Warehouse were African American, and 60 percent of those at Diamond Toys were white. Only three African Americans, all women, worked at

Diamond Toys. No black men worked at that store. In contrast, only four white women (including me) worked at the Toy Warehouse. In this chapter, I explore the reasons for this and other dramatic differences in the organization of these toy stores.

Sociologists have long recognized the workplace as a central site for the reproduction of social inequalities. Studies of factory work in particular have shown us how race and gender hierarchies are reproduced through the social organization of the work.[4] I argue that the labor process in service industries is equally important for understanding social inequality, even though this sector has not come under the same degree of scrutiny by sociologists.[5] I demonstrate how the working conditions at the two stores perpetuate inequality by class, gender, and race. The jobs are organized in such a way as to benefit some groups of workers and discriminate against others.

The stores where I worked represent a range of working conditions in large retail trade establishments. Although both were affiliated with national chains and both were in the business of selling toys, Diamond Toys was unionized and the Toy Warehouse was not. The union protected workers from some of the most egregious aspects of retail work. But, as I will show, the union could not overcome the race, gender, and class inequalities that are reproduced by the social organization of the industry.

STRATIFIED SELLING

Diamond Toys and the Toy Warehouse each employed about seventy workers. As in other large retail establishments, the workers were organized in an elaborate hierarchy. Each store was governed by a regional office, which in turn was overseen by the national corporate headquarters. There was no local autonomy in the layout or the merchandise sold in the stores. Within each store, directors were at the top, followed by managers, supervisors, and associates. Directors and managers were salaried employees; everyone else was hourly. Most directors and managers had a college degree. Candidates for these jobs applied to the regional headquarters and, once hired, were assigned to specific stores. These might not be the stores closest to where they lived. Olive, my manager at the Toy Warehouse, had a two-hour commute each way to work, even though there was a Toy Warehouse within five miles of her home.

The hierarchy of jobs and power within the stores was marked by race and gender. In both stores the directors and assistant directors were white men. Immediately below them were managers, who were a more diverse group, including men and women, whites and Latinas/os, and, at the Toy Warehouse, an African American woman (Olive). There were far more managers at Diamond Toys than at the Toy Warehouse; I met at least ten managers during my time there, versus only two at the Toy Warehouse.

The next layer of the hierarchy under managers were supervisors, who were drawn from the ranks of associates. They were among those who had the most seniority and thus the most knowledge of store procedures, and they had limited authority to do things like void transactions at the registers. All of the supervisors at Diamond Toys were white and most were men, while at the Toy Warehouse supervisors were more racially diverse and most were women. It took me a long time to figure out who the supervisors were at the Toy Warehouse. Many of those I thought were supervisors turned out to be regular employees. They had many of the same responsibilities as supervisors, but, as I came to find out, they were competing with each other for promotion to this position. When I asked why they were acting like supervisors, it was explained to me that the Toy Warehouse wouldn't promote anyone before he or she was proficient at the higher job. This policy justified giving workers more responsibilities without more pay. At Diamond Toys, in contrast, job descriptions were clearer and were enforced.

Associates were the largest group of workers at the stores (sometimes referred to as the staff). They included men and women of all races and ethnic groups and different ages, except at Diamond Toys, where I noted that there were no black men. Despite the apparent diversity among the staff, there was substantial segregation by race and gender in the tasks they were assigned. Employees of toy stores are divided between back- and front-of-house workers. The back-of-house employees and managers work in the storage areas, on the loading docks, and in the assembly rooms. In both stores where I worked, the back-of-house workers were virtually all men. The front-of-house workers, the ones who interacted with customers, included both men and women. But there, too, there was job segregation by gender and race, although, as I will discuss, it was harder to discern and on occasion it broke down.

There were two other jobs in the toy store: security guards and janitors, both of whom were subcontracted workers. Both the Toy Warehouse and Diamond Toys employed plainclothes security guards who watched surveillance monitors in their back offices and roamed the aisles looking for shoplifters. At the Toy Warehouse, the individuals who filled those jobs were mostly African American men and women, while only white men and women were hired for security at Diamond Toys. Finally, all of the cleaners at the two stores were Latinas. They were recent immigrants who didn't speak English.

What accounts for the race and gender segregation of jobs in the toy store? Conventional economic theory argues that job segregation is the product of differences in human capital attainment. According to this view, the marketplace sorts workers into jobs depending on their qualifications and preferences. Because men and women of different racial/ethnic groups possess different skills, aptitudes, and work experiences, they will be (and indeed should be) hired into different jobs. Economists generally see this process as benign, if not beneficial, in a society founded on meritocracy, individual liberty, and freedom of choice (Folbre 2001).

In contrast, when sociologists look at job segregation, they tend to see discrimination and structural inequality (Reskin and Roos 1990). Obtaining the right qualifications for a high-paying job is easier for some groups than others. Differential access to college education is an obvious example: society blocks opportunities for poor people to acquire this human capital asset while smoothing the path for the well-to-do. But the sociological critique of job segregation goes deeper than this. Sociologists argue that the definitions of who is qualified and what it means to be qualified for a job are linked to stereotypes about race and gender. Joan Acker (1990) argues that jobs are "gendered," meaning that qualities culturally associated with men (leadership, physical strength, aggression, goal orientation) are built into the job descriptions of the higher-status and higher-paid occupations in our economy. Qualities associated with women (dexterity, passivity, nurturing orientation) tend to be favored in low-paying jobs. In addition to being gendered, jobs are racialized. Black women have been subjected to a different set of gendered stereotypes than white women. Far from being seen as delicate and passive, they have been perceived as dominant, insubordinate, and aggressive (Collins 2000). Those who make hiring decisions draw upon these kinds of racialized stereotypes of masculinity and femininity when appointing workers to specific jobs.

Leslie Salzinger (2003) has examined how this job placement works in manufacturing plants along the U.S.-Mexico border. She uses the concept of "interpellation" to describe how managers imagine a specific, embodied worker in each job and how workers come to see themselves in these imaginings. Workers, in other words, typically consent to and embrace the stereotypes, since their opportunities depend on their conformity to these managerial imaginings. She shows that to get a job on the assembly line, young women workers have to represent themselves as docile, dexterous, and unencumbered by family responsibilities. They really have no choice: to get a job they must become the embodiment of their bosses' stereotypes. Eventually, she argues, the line between the stereotype and the authentic self blurs.

This process may be exacerbated in interactive service work, where employers carefully pick workers who "look right" for the corporate image they attempt to project to the public. A recent court case against Abercrombie & Fitch illustrates this. A suit was brought against the retailer by Asian Americans and Latinas/os who said they were refused selling jobs because "they didn't project what the company called the A & F look" (Greenhouse 2003). Although the company denied the charge, the suit brings to light the common retail practice of matching employees with the image the company is seeking to cultivate. More egregious examples are found in sexualized service work, as in the case of Hooters restaurants (where only buxom young women are hired), and in theme parks like Disney, notorious for its resistance to hiring African Americans (Loe 1996; Project on Disney 1995).

This process of interpellation was apparent in the toy stores where I worked: managers imagined different kinds of people in each job, who came to see themselves in terms of these stereotypical expectations. Because these jobs involved interacting with customers, managers also considered the public's expectations when making job assignments, which were not an issue in the factories studied by Salzinger. Furthermore, I observed far more worker resistance than Salzinger found in her study, especially at the Toy Warehouse. Ultimately, I maintain, job segregation in retail work reflects the dynamic outcome of conflict between workers' desires, managers' interests, and customers' expectations.

My experience illustrates this process of interpellation and resistance. I was hired to be a cashier at both toy stores. I didn't seek out this job, but this was how both managers who hired me envisioned my potential contribution. Only women were regularly assigned to work as cashiers at the Toy Warehouse, and I noticed that management preferred young or light-skinned women for this job. Some older African American women who wanted to work as cashiers had to struggle to get the assignment. Lazelle, for example, who was about thirty-five, had been asking to be put on register over the two months she had been working there. She had been assigned to be a merchandiser. Merchandisers retrieved items from the storeroom, priced items, and checked prices when the universal product codes (UPCs) were missing. Lazelle finally got her chance at the register the same day that I started. We set up next to each other, and I noticed with a bit of envy how much more competent and confident on the register she was compared to me. (Later she told me she had worked registers at other stores, including fast-food restaurants.) I told her that I had been hoping to get assigned to the job of merchandiser. I liked the idea of being free to walk around the store, engage with customers, and learn more about the toys. I had mentioned to Olive that I wanted that job, but she had made it clear that I was destined for cashiering and the service desk (and later, to my horror, computer account-ing). Lazelle looked at me as if I were crazy. Merchandising was generally considered to be the worst job in the store because it was so physically taxing. From her point of view I had been as-signed the better job, no doubt because of my race, and it seemed to her that I wanted to throw that advantage away.[6]

The preference for whites in the cashier position reflected the importance of this job in the store's general operations. In dis-count stores like the Toy Warehouse, customers had few oppor-tunities to interact and consult with salesclerks. As I will discuss in chapter 4, most shoppers at the Toy Warehouse knew they were on their own in the stores and rarely asked salesclerks for their ad-vice on purchases. The cashier was the only human being that the customer was guaranteed to contact, giving the role enormous symbolic—and economic—importance for the organization. At the point of sale, transactions could break down if the customers were not treated in accordance with their expectations. The pref-erence for white and light-skinned women as cashiers should be interpreted in this light: in a racist and sexist society, such women are generally believed to be the friendliest and most solicitous group and thus best able to inspire trust and confidence.[7]

Personally, I hated working as a cashier. I thought it was a dif-ficult, stressful, and thankless job. Learning to work a cash register is much like learning to use a new computer software package. Each store seems to use a different operating system. After working at these jobs I started to pay attention to every transaction that I made as a customer in a store, and I have yet to see the same computer system twice. The job looks simple from the outside, but because of the way it is organized cashiers have no discretionary power, making them completely dependent on others if anything out of the ordinary happens. Like every large store, the places where I worked used UPCs on the merchandise, and we scanned these with a laser instead of entering prices into the register. Managers had a special key that they could use to override the UPC, but the cashiers did not, which caused a great deal of frustration to customers. If the customer knew the price of an item but the UPC tag was missing, we would have to search for the item in the inventory code book (at Diamond Toys) or page a merchandiser (at the Toy Warehouse) to go find another one with the tag in place so we could scan it into the register. If customers changed their minds midtransaction, we would have to call a manager to void their purchase. If they asked for a small discount on damaged merchandise, we had to ask the manager. If they didn't have the money to cover a purchase, the register would freeze up and we would have to call the manager. We couldn't even open up our registers to make change for the gum ball machine. Customers would often treat us like morons because we couldn't resolve these minor and routine situations on our own, but we were given no choice or autonomy.

We were, however, held accountable for everything in the register, which had to match the computer printout record of all transactions. At the Toy Warehouse, we were also responsible for requesting "pulls" (this was done automatically by the security personnel at Diamond Toys). A pull is when a manager removes large sums of cash from the register to protect the money in case of a robbery. We were told to request a pull whenever we accumulated more than $500 cash in our registers. If we didn't, and large sums of money were in the till when we closed out our registers at the end of the shift, we would be given a demerit. Interestingly, we were never given any instruction on what to do to protect ourselves in case of an actual robbery.

Talwar (2002) notes in her study of fast-food restaurants that African American men are sometimes preferred as cashiers during the nighttime hours, especially in dangerous neighborhoods. This is presumed to offer some protection for the registers in case of attempted robbery. Here again we see how the image of "cashier" is linked to managers' race and gender stereotypes regarding the qualifications for the job. At the Toy Warehouse, African American men were not routinely assigned to the register at any time of day or night, but they were used to perform a security function in the evening. When the store closed at the end of the day, Olive would make an announcement over the public intercom instructing two black men to "clear the store" and "check the bathrooms." This was often said in a menacing way to scare the stragglers into leaving, especially if it had to be repeated more than once. This task assignment drew upon and bolstered stereotypes about the strength and inherent aggressiveness of African American men.

Cashiers did perform some security tasks at the Toy Warehouse. In addition to being responsible for requesting pulls, we were expected to check the customers' bags and receipts whenever the alarm sounded at the front door. The alarm was set off when people left the store with merchandise affixed with security tags that had not been properly deactivated. This happened approximately every ten minutes. Half of the people who set off the alarm turned around immediately to offer proof that they were not guilty of anything, and the other half just continued walking out the door. We tended to ignore both groups. We were usually too busy with other customers to stop and check the ones who came back into the store, so we just waved them out. We certainly were not going to run after customers who continued walking out. If they had indeed stolen any merchandise, we weren't about to expose ourselves to the potential danger of a physical confrontation. I thought that this should have been the job of a uniformed security force, but Olive told me that a uniformed guard would damage the store's image as a welcoming and happy place.

A few men were regularly assigned to work as cashiers at the Toy Warehouse, but this happened only in the electronics department. The electronics department was cordoned off from the rest of the store by a metal detector gate intended to curtail theft. All of the men with this regular assignment were Asian American. They had sought out this assignment because they were interested in computers and gaming equipment. Working a register in that section may have been more acceptable to them in part because the section was separated from the main registers and in part because Asian masculinity—as opposed to black or white masculinity—is often defined through technical expertise. My sense was that the stereotypical association of Asian American men with computers made these assignments desirable from management's perspective as well.

Occasionally men were assigned to work the registers outside the electronics department, but this happened only when there were staffing shortages or scheduling problems. Once I came to work to find Deshay, a twenty-five-year-old African American, and Shuresh, a twenty-one-year-old second-generation Indian American, both stationed at the main registers. I flew to the back of the store to clock in so I could take my station next to them, eager to observe them negotiating the demands of "women's work." But the minute I took my station they were relieved of cashiering and told to cash out their registers and return to their regular tasks. When a woman was available, the men didn't have to do the job.

On a previous occasion, I had observed Deshay skillfully evade the assignment to work register. Deshay normally worked as a merchandiser, and he also worked in the storeroom unloading boxes from the delivery trucks. I noticed when he was called to the register because I had never seen an African American man work there. Olive called Deshay to her office over the walkie-talkie (without telling him why—if he had known why, he later told me, he wouldn't have responded to the page). Next thing I saw him with a register drawer, and he was told to start counting it out in preparation for cashiering. He took the till over to the service desk, and I turned around for a moment and he was gone! Eventually I caught up with him in the break room and asked him what happened. I said, "That was some disappearing act!" He told me, with mounting exasperation and anger, that he did not want to work register, he was not hired to work register, he had too many other jobs to do, and if they forced him to work register he would file a lawsuit against them. He didn't say outright that cashiering was a lousy job, my guess is, because that was the job I was doing.

This is another example of interpellation. Deshay had come to see himself in managerial stereotypes about the appropriate roles for black men. But I think that another reason Deshay didn't want to cashier was that he felt his masculinity was at stake. For many men, work functions as outward proof of their masculine identity (Williams 1989, 1995). Their poise, their sense of strength, and even their heterosexuality are challenged when they do "women's work." Even though there is nothing inherently feminine about working a cash register, management had defined the job as "women's work," and Deshay was eager to distance himself from any job considered "feminine." This psychological incentive fit in with managerial goals. In this way, workplaces draw on gender to "manufacture consent"—that is, to make workers complicit in the social organization that management prefers.

On another occasion of "crossing over" at the Toy Warehouse, Jack, a heavily tattooed forty-year-old white supervisor, had to cover the baby registry (usually a "woman's job") when the regular worker went on break. This was a computer station near the rear of the store where pregnant women planning their baby showers could go and make a "wish list" of gifts they wanted to receive from their friends and family. Jack tried very hard to resist this assignment but had no choice in the end. When I heard his voice crackle over the walkie-talkie asking where he could find the baby booties, I thought he was going to die of humiliation.

The stores exploited young men's insecurity in their masculinity by assigning them to jobs that required them to do a great deal of heavy lifting. They had to move freight and deliver large items (like baby car seats, play sets, and bikes) to the front of the store and occasionally out to the customer's car. Several men told me that the physical aspect of their work wore them out and meant that their jobs in retail could only be temporary. But at the same time they took a great deal of pride in these tasks. Because the tasks were defined as masculine, they seemed to experience a boost in self-esteem for accomplishing them.

Women also crossed over into the men's jobs, but this happened far less frequently. Management never assigned a woman to work in the back areas to make up for temporary staff shortfalls. At each store, only one woman worked in the back of the house, and both women were African American. At the Toy Warehouse, the only woman who worked in the back was Darlene, whom a coworker once described to me as "very masculine" (but also "really great"). Darlene, who worked in a contracting business on the side, took a lot of pride in her physical strength and stamina. She was also a lesbian, which made her the butt of mean-spirited joking (behind her back) but also probably made this assignment less dissonant in the eyes of management (women in nontraditional jobs are often stereotyped as lesbian). At Diamond Toys, the only woman in the back of the house was eighteen-year-old Chandrika. She started working in the back of the house but asked for and received a transfer to gift wrap. Chandrika, who was one of only three African Americans who worked at Diamond Toys, said she hated working in the storeroom because the men there were racist and "very misogynistic," telling sexist jokes and challenging her competence at the job.

Crossing over is a different experience for men and women. When a job is identified as masculine, men often will erect barriers to women, making them feel out of place and unwanted, which is what happened to Chandrika. In contrast, I never observed women trying to exclude men or marginalize men in "their" jobs. On the contrary, men tried to exclude themselves from "women's work." Job segregation by gender is in large part a product of men's efforts to establish all-male preserves, which help them to prove and to maintain their masculinity (Williams 1989). Management colludes in this insofar as they share similar stereotypes of appropriate task assignments for men and women or perceive the public to embrace such stereotypes. But they also insist on employee "flexibility," the widespread euphemism used to describe their fundamental right to hire, fire, and assign employees at will. At the Toy Warehouse, employees were often threatened that their hours would be cut if they were not "flexible" in terms of their available hours and willingness to perform any job. But in general managers shared men's preferences to avoid register duty unless no one else was available.

How and why a specific job comes to be "gendered" and "racialized," or considered appropriate only for women or for men, or for whites or nonwhites, depends on the specific context (which in the case of these toy stores was shaped—but not determined—by their national marketing strategies, discussed in chapter 4). Thus, in contrast to the Toy Warehouse, Diamond Toys employed both men and women as cashiers, and only two of them were African American (both women). At the Toy Warehouse, most of the registers were lined up in the front of the store near the doors. Diamond Toys was more like a department store with cash registers scattered throughout the different sections. The preference for white workers seemed consistent with the marketing of the store's workers as "the ultimate toy experts." In retail service work, professional expertise is typically associated with whiteness, much as it is in domestic service (Wrigley 1995).

Although both men and women worked the registers, there was gender segregation by the type of toy we sold. Only women were assigned to work in the doll and stuffed animal sections, for example, and only men worked in sporting goods and electronics. Also, only women worked in gift wrap. Some sections, like the book department, were gender neutral, but most were as gender marked as the toys we sold.

This gender segregation occasionally would break down at Diamond Toys, and men would be assigned to work in the women's sections when enough women weren't available. At Diamond Toys, Carl, a thirty-year-old white man, once had to work backup with me in dolls. He performed the role in a completely campy style, swishing around the floor and answering the phone with "Barbie speaking!" Carl, who normally didn't act this way, was parodying the assumed homosexuality of any man interested in dolls (and, indeed, many of the high-end Barbie customers were gay). Turning the role into a joke made his temporary assignment seem more palatable and less inconsistent with his masculinity.

The most firmly segregated job in the toy store was the job of cleaner. As I have noted, only Latinas filled these jobs. I never witnessed a man or a woman of different race/ethnicity in them. (The reasons for the segregation of Latinas into cleaning jobs have been explored by Hondagneu-Sotelo [2001].) There were different degrees of integration and acceptance of the cleaners at the two stores. Estella, who was the only cleaner at the Toy Warehouse, was well integrated among the associates. The staff appreciated the hard work she did: it was, after all, a truly Herculean effort to keep that store clean. In contrast, the three Latina cleaners at Diamond Toys seemed alienated from the rest of the staff. Few people ever talked to them. I thought at first that this was because most of the associates couldn't speak Spanish, but I noticed that hardly anyone even said hello. I would often observe them in the break room sitting alone with no one to talk to. Angie, a twenty-seven-year-old Latina associate, told me that she thought people

were mean to the cleaners and ignored them because they were
Hispanic. Because I spoke Spanish I could break that norm. In
fact, once I was talking to Rosario, a cleaner from Costa Rica, and
Lisa, a twenty-five-year-old Latina who worked in the back office,
walked by. She looked startled and asked me if I spoke Spanish. I
said yes, and she said, "But I thought you were, uh, white." It
amazed her that a white person could and would speak to the janitors. In addition to preserving masculinity, then, job segregation
helped to preserve the privileges of whiteness. Ignoring the cleaners promoted a status distinction between "their" jobs and the
work of "regular" employees.

HOURS, BENEFITS, AND PAY

When I started this project I thought I had the perfect career to
combine with a part-time job in retail. As a college professor, I
taught two courses per semester that met six hours per week. I
thought I could pick a schedule for twenty hours a week that accommodated those teaching commitments. Wrong. To get a job
in retail, workers must be willing to work weekends and to change
their schedules from one week to another to meet the staffing
needs of the store. This is the meaning of the word *flexible* in retail. It is exactly the kind of schedule that is incompatible with
doing anything else.

Retail is often marketed as a great part-time work opportunity
because of the "flexible" schedules. Mothers looking to combine
work with their primary family responsibilities are drawn to these
jobs. I met a mother of three preschool children at a job fair with
this goal in mind. She and I met in a seminar room with four others who were applying for a job at a children's warehouse store.

Before the formal presentation started, we talked about why we were there. She told me that she preferred not to work, that she valued her role as full-time wife and mother, and that she would never put her kids in day care. But she had decided to get a job because of an argument she had had with her husband. She had recently asked him to buy her a cell phone. He had told her that if she really wanted a cell phone, she should get a job. So she had decided to look for a retail job for the hours 5:00 to 10:00 P.M. She had picked those hours because her husband would be home from work then and thus available to look after the children. He'd also have to feed them and put them to bed, she noted with a devious smile.

I didn't get that job, and I suspect that she didn't either. We wanted flexible jobs, but the store wanted flexible workers. I learned from my experience to never limit the hours I would work on job applications. Giant retailers do not cater to the needs of employees; their goal is to hire a constant stream of entry-level, malleable, and replaceable workers. This organizational preference for high turnover keeps labor costs down (Talwar 2002).

Workers with seniority can gain some control over their schedules, but it takes years of "flexibility" to attain to this status. Moreover, in my experience, this control was guaranteed only at Diamond Toys, thanks to the union. The senior associates who had worked there more than a year had the same schedule from week to week. This didn't apply to the supervisors, though. They had to be willing to fill in as needed, since there had to be a supervisor on the floor at all times. Occasionally they even had to forgo breaks.

The fact that supervisors had less control over their schedules made the job less desirable, but to sweeten the pot the job paid $1 per hour more than what regular associates earned. From the perspective of at least two women senior associates I talked to, it just wasn't worth it to give up control over their schedules. But this effectively prevented them from rising in the hierarchy and making more money, and it contributed to the gender segregation of jobs.

What did people earn? At Diamond Toys we were instructed during our training session not to discuss our pay with anyone. Doing so was pointed out as an example of "unauthorized disclosure of confidential business information," a "serious willful violation" that could result in immediate discharge. So I wasn't about to ask anyone what he or she made. I made $8.75 per hour. I got a sense that that was about average but somewhat higher than what most new hires made (possibly because of my higher educational credentials).

To put this salary into perspective, a forty-hour, full-time, year-round worker making $8.75 per hour would earn about $17,500 before taxes. This was well above the median income of full-time cashiers in 2001, which was about $15,000 per year, and about average for retail sales workers in general, who earned a median income of $18,000 (U.S. Bureau of Labor Statistics 2003). Of course, most retail workers do not work full time and year round, so their incomes are much lower than this.

I asked my supervisor Dennis how much associates *could* make, maximum. He said he wasn't sure. I suggested perhaps $15? He said that he had never known anyone to make that much. I talked to another coworker, Brad, about pay. Brad was a young white man, about twenty-three, who had worked at Diamond Toys a few years earlier and then quit during his probationary period (ninety days) and moved to Orlando. He had gotten a job there at another Diamond Toys, where he had worked for a couple of years, eventually becoming a supervisor. But he had decided that he hated Orlando, so he had moved back to this store three months ago. His supervisor position didn't transfer, but his wages did, he said. I said that sounded all right. He said he didn't know how his wages compared with the beginning wages at our store, and he joked that he didn't *want* to know, so I jumped in and told him that I made $8.75. He said he didn't make much more than that, and his last raise was 50 cents per hour!

As this store was located in a major urban area with very high rents and real estate prices, I was curious about how people managed to survive on such low wages. Ordinances passed in 2001 in the two cities where I worked set the "living wage" (with benefits) at about $10 per hour. Brad told me he lived at a youth hostel in a room above a nightclub that he shared with three other guys. He paid only $90 per week (which worked out to be about 25 percent of his income if he worked full time). He loved it, he said, especially meeting new people, plus they all got free admission into the club. I couldn't help but laugh, thinking that living above a noisy club wouldn't be my idea of a good time, but maybe it would have been when I was twenty-three.

Those who didn't live in the city faced long and often grueling commutes. When I first met Mario, a twenty-five-year-old Latino, he was trying to take a nap on one of the ratty couches in the break room. It was almost 9:00 A.M., the start of my shift, and I asked him when he was on. He told me that his shift didn't start until noon but that he had had to come in early to get a ride with his sister, Angie, who was working 9:00 to 5:00. They lived in a suburb about thirty-five miles away. He explained that it took about two and a half hours to get to work by public transportation, so he figured he came out ahead (and saved some money) by coming in three hours early. When he had first been hired at Diamond Toys he lived in the city, but he had moved out to the suburbs about a year ago and there were no jobs there as good as this one. He said he had just found out that he had to have work done on a tooth, probably a root canal, and that it was going to cost $2,000, but it was all going to be paid for, thanks to the union benefits. So the job—with the long commute—was worth it to him.

Not everyone liked the union, since dues were $30 per month, about a day's pay for most part-time workers. Brad didn't like the union for this reason, but since it was a closed shop at this particular store, everyone had to belong.

Most of the young white associates in the store were single, going to college or making plans to do so, and living in group settings. The young Latina/o and Asian American associates mostly lived at home with their parents. The older white employees were married or partnered and had a variety of backgrounds, including some out-of-work actors, a few who had worked for failed dot-coms, and even an attorney. Carl had just moved to the city with his wife and had taken the job (plus a second one doing part-time legal work) to tide himself over as he prepared to take the bar exam. The presence of these underemployed professionals on the sales floor seemed to be demoralizing to the long-term workers and served as an incentive to stay on the job. In a recession, workers may put up with unfavorable working conditions in the interests of keeping secure employment.

Interestingly, no one at Diamond Toys appeared to have any children. I asked Dennis about this, and he verified that no one had children that he could think of, a fact he attributed to their youth and their attendance at college. Several gay men worked at the store (at the managerial level), another possible reason behind the childlessness. I did meet one young associate who had a six-year-old daughter, but I later learned that the daughter lived with her father in another state. The complete absence of parents suggests a systematic bias in the hiring and/or retention of workers. Perhaps those with child care responsibilities were less able to conform to the "flexible" requirements of the job.

This was a huge contrast to my experience at the Toy Warehouse, where most of my women coworkers were single mothers. I met only three other women aside from myself who didn't have children. (Interestingly, those three others were full-time employees at the supervisory level.) Most of the men also had children. Here the systematic bias was in favor of hiring parents. This was in part a consequence of the fact that the Toy Warehouse participated in the "workfare" program, whereby businesses that hired welfare recipients could receive reimbursement for part of their wages. Since welfare was designed to provide aid to families with dependent children, all recipients had children. All new hires (including me) were given a form to certify their employment for the welfare office. These forms were also used by the store to obtain a federal reimbursement under the "work opportunity tax credit." This tax credit, part of the welfare reform of 1996, reimbursed businesses for 35 percent of wages for the first year and 50 percent the second, to a maximum of $8,500 per new hire (qualified wages were capped at $10,000 per year). Participating in the program helped the Toy Warehouse cut down significantly on its labor costs.[8]

The unpredictability of scheduling presented a nightmare for many single mothers at the Toy Warehouse. Schedules were posted on Friday for the following week beginning on Sunday. The two-day notice of scheduling made it especially difficult to arrange child care. (In contrast, schedules came out on Tuesday for the following week at Diamond Toys, another benefit of the union.) Even worse, while I was working at the Toy Warehouse, management reduced everyone's hours, purportedly to make up for revenue shortfalls. We were all asked to fill in a form indicating our "availability" to work, from 6:00 A.M. until 10:00 P.M. This form, which was attached to our paychecks, warned that "associates with the flexible availability will get more hours than those who are limited." Part-timers who limited their availability were hit hard when schedules came out the following week, causing a great deal of anger and bad feelings. Angela, an experienced associate, was scheduled for only four hours, and she was so mad that no one could even talk to her. Some said that they were going to apply for unemployment. Deshay offered to get me the phone number for the county unemployment office because I was given only 13.5 hours, well below the 20 he told me was the maximum one could work in order to qualify for unemployment benefits.[9]

One of the reasons management gave for cutting our hours was that the store had been experiencing major problems with "shrink," the retailer term for theft. It was insinuated that the workers were stealing, but I could never figure out how that could happen. In both stores, very elaborate surveillance systems were set up to monitor employees. Hidden cameras recorded activity throughout the store, including the areas around the emergency exits. Our bags, pockets, and purses were checked every time we left the store. Cashiers were monitored continuously via a backroom computer hooked up to every register. As I noted, the contents of the till had to match exactly with the register report. Being even slightly under was enough to cause a major panic.

This happened once to Esme, an African American woman in

her thirties who had worked for the Toy Warehouse for fifteen years. I was in the counting room with Esme when she came up $6 short. She was devastated by this. I said to Doris, the supervisor, that I hated working on register for this reason. Six dollars seemed so insignificant; it seemed wrong that a good employee was beating herself up over it. Doris said that was because Esme had worked there for so long with a perfect record, and I said, "Precisely, that's right, people should cut her some slack if she comes up short occasionally; it's no big deal to the company after all." Doris didn't say anything, but then she rarely said anything. Esme's job was on the line and we knew it.

Even if some employees were stealing, I thought it was counterproductive to cut back on staffing to make up for revenue shortfalls. But big box retailers probably would like to do away with service workers altogether. The historical trend in retail has been to train customers in "self-serve" (Glazer 1993). Some stores today are trying to go the way of gas stations, where customers scan their own merchandise, insert a credit card to purchase it, and bag it themselves. I imagine that the surveillance systems must be quite elaborate in these stores. But even with sophisticated technologies, someone has to be employed to watch the monitors, and more have to be ready to intervene if "shrink" is occurring. It seems unlikely that surveillance systems will ever completely replace service workers for this reason.

Eliminating service workers is probably more a retailer's fantasy than future for another reason: for many consumers, shopping is an interactive experience. At the high-end Diamond Toys it was dogma that customers all desired to engage with service workers, where we received training in the "Five I's" of customer service (Initiate, Inquire, Inform, Include, and Into the Register).

But even at the Toy Warehouse, managers knew that service workers helped to produce happy and satisfied customers. They emphasized to us that repeat business depended on the customer's favorable experience with the workers, especially with the cashiers. Mark, the store director of the Toy Warehouse, kept urging us to smile at the customers, whom we were required to call "guests."

To reward us for good customer service, the Toy Warehouse management would occasionally give us "toy bucks," scriplike coupons redeemable for a Coke or an ice cream bar. The coupons were given for a variety of reasons, including "never letting a guest leave our store dissatisfied" and "thanking guests and inviting them to return." Once after an especially busy day, the entire closing staff got a toy buck, prompting one of my coworkers to remark cynically, "How many of these does it take to get a TV?"

Toy bucks were miserly rewards, but they did improve the morale of some workers, who, after all, were making very miserly incomes. The Toy Warehouse paid less than Diamond Toys. I earned $7.50 per hour, which I later found out was a relatively high starting salary. Pak Chew, who was hired at the same time I was, made only $7.10, but this was his first job ever. Later Pak Chew was offered a full-time job at UPS for $11 per hour, and to his and everyone's amazement, Mark offered him $9 to stay (he didn't).

There weren't rules against discussing wages at the Toy Warehouse, but most workers avoided the topic. It was an embarrassing subject, especially if it was revealed that some people (especially the new hires) earned more than the longer-term employees. I learned that some of my coworkers who had been at the store much longer made the same wage that I did. Vern, a fifty-year-old black man who had worked in bike assembly for two years, was distressed to learn that Paul, a new hire, was making as much as he was, even though Vern had just received a 25-cent raise. Paul, a twenty-two-year-old heavily tattooed white man, was hired for $8 per hour. Paul told me this when I first met him in the break room. He complained about his low wage and announced that in one month he would demand a raise to $9. He explained that his father was a good friend of Jack, the supervisor of the bike department. That was how he had gotten this job, along with the promise that he would be making more money.

Paul was one exception to the norm of not talking about wages, and it didn't make him any friends. Most thought he was a braggart and avoided him. Another exception was Michelle, a thirty-three-year-old African American woman. Michelle talked about wages and working conditions at every opportunity, but she was enormously popular and well liked. One day before my shift I was in the break room when Michelle arrived. She was furious because her paycheck didn't reflect the overtime she had been forced to work the previous Saturday when the staff had been required to come to an unscheduled meeting. (The issue of unpaid overtime is the subject of class action lawsuits brought against Wal-Mart. See Greenhouse 2002.) Other employees said that they were going to make a point of noticing whether they were also shorted on their paychecks. Then Michelle started singing wonderful made-up rap songs about our lousy jobs and the whole break room erupted with laughter and shouting.

One of the issues that Michelle raised was that the new people (including me) were taking the established people's hours. None of the new workers were African American (we were white, Asian American, and Latina), and this formed an unspoken backdrop to her complaint. Michelle had tried to get a petition drive going to complain about the diminishing hours, but no one would sign her petition. She was very frustrated. People told her, "I don't want to lose my job; I need this job." Well, so did she, but who would fight for their rights, she wanted to know. She didn't involve the new people in the organizing, but she complained to me later that the others were not brave enough to fight for their rights. They talked a good deal in the break room, she said, but when push came to shove they were not there to support her and her campaign for better working conditions.

Michelle was one of several workers who had two jobs. Nationally, about 6 percent of all workers hold two jobs (Amirault 1997), but nearly every associate I met at the Toy Warehouse also worked someplace else to supplement his or her income. Michelle worked for the school district as a janitor, making about $11 per hour. She had started at the Toy Warehouse at Christmastime, when school was out, and Olive had asked her to stay on. She had explained about her other job, and Olive had promised to work around it, but as it turned out that didn't happen. She complained that sometimes she was asked to be at work at noon, but her other job required her to be there until 1:30, so how could she make it on time? Then she was written up for being late, which seemed totally unfair to her. She said she had two demerits against her which she had been called into the main office to sign, and she had said no, she didn't agree that she was in the wrong. She had been told that the demerits would go in her file anyway, and she had said, "Then what's the point of signing?"

Michelle was also upset because her perceived insubordination resulted in her being demoted to cashier. She had been working at the service desk, a position with more authority and more varied responsibilities but not more pay. The service desk worker could clear voided transactions and open registers to make change and pull out large amounts of cash to put into the safe. A person in this position wore register keys around her neck, a symbolic marker of her higher authority and status (only women were ever assigned this job). Michelle was furious to be assigned to a register, a situation made worse by the fact that the person assigned to service desk was new at the job and had to ask Michelle how to perform most of her tasks.

Michelle was so frustrated that she eventually decided to resign. She composed her letter of resignation at the register next to mine, so we talked about it while she was working on it. The letter was addressed to Mark, the store director, who had replaced the former director in charge when Michelle was hired. She told me (in the break room with the others) that when she had been hired she had been promised $10 per hour, which she thought was OK combined with her other job at $11. But then she found out she would be getting only $9.25, which she thought was insulting, given her prior experience at Kmart. (One of the others backed her up and said that anything she was promised by the previous director was probably not honored, since he often lied to employees.) When she confronted the managers about this they said that this was standard but that after three months there would be a 25- to 50-cent raise. When her three months came up she was given 25 cents, which set her off. In fact, the very first time I met Michelle she was carrying on in the break room, shouting that she was going to tell the manager to shove that 25 cents up her ass.

TAKE THIS JOB AND SHOVE IT—OR NOT

Over the course of working at the two stores, I witnessed a great deal of employee turnover. I outlasted both of the others who were hired with me at the Toy Warehouse, and by the time I left Diamond Toys I was the third in seniority among the ten associates who worked in my section. On one of my last days there I was given the walkie-talkie, the direct line of communication to the storeroom and the managers' office, which indicated that I was at that time the most senior staff member in the section.

For most employees, retail work is a revolving door.[10] Employers know this and expect and even cultivate it. Most new hires are not expected to last through the three-month probation period. One of my coworkers at the Toy Warehouse told me he rarely talked to the new people since they rarely lasted long. Kevin, a twenty-six-year-old African American supervisor, predicted I wouldn't stay very long because I didn't have the right personality for retail work. I asked him, "What kind of people stay at the store?" He said people who were quiet and didn't stress out easily (my major flaw), and then he whispered, "People who can kiss up to management." I asked him, did he do this? And he said yes, but in a different kind of way, not too obvious. I asked how, and he said that he didn't tell people what he "really" thought if he thought he was being screwed over.

Kevin was one of a handful of hourly workers who saw their jobs at the Toy Warehouse as their lifelong work. He told me that he had "grown up" at the Toy Warehouse and could never imagine leaving. There were also a half-dozen or so associates at Diamond Toys who had worked at the store for more than a year. It is much more understandable why workers might choose to stay there, given the union benefits. An extra incentive for staying was the possibility of moving into management. At least a third of the managers at Diamond Toys started working as regular associates. When they became managers they left the union and earned salaries, starting at about $35,000. In contrast, no associate ever moved into management at the Toy Warehouse, although one of my young coworkers maintained that it *could* happen. Vannie, a twenty-one-year-old first-generation immigrant from the Philippines, told me that she had met someone at another store in the chain (which had since closed down) who knew someone who had worked his way up from janitor to store director. I told her that I thought this seemed unlikely. Janitorial services were subcontracted, and director and management positions required a college degree and involved a completely separate application process through the regional office in another state. The story sounded like a Horatio Alger myth to me. But Vannie said that this man was a great inspiration to her, and I believed her.

Although acquiring a management position at Diamond Toys wasn't unprecedented, few of the long-term associates seemed interested in pursuing one. Some seemed resigned to keeping their associate position with its guaranteed hours, schedule, and benefits. Alyss, for example, had worked two years in the doll department and had a set schedule from 8:00 to 4:30, five days per week. She told me she couldn't believe she had worked at the store that long but that at this point she considered the job pretty easy. The only drawbacks were her dealings with Dorothy (the irritable section manager) and the occasional neurotic high-end Barbie collector. She had no interest in pursuing a supervisory position because that would mean losing her schedule and taking on more work.

Alyss and the other long-timers didn't exactly like their jobs, but they had become experts in the work, which was no small feat. Barbara Ehrenreich (2001) writes that there is no such thing as an unskilled job, an observation that I confirmed during my first two weeks at each of the two toy stores. Every store does things differently, so the first days on the job are a nightmare. Very little training is given, which is not surprising given the high turnover, but the result is that a new worker can feel like a complete buffoon. At my jobs, doing the simplest things, like locating the proper place to put a toy back on the shelf, could take ages to accomplish and was not unlike finding one piece in a jigsaw puzzle. I once spent twenty minutes trying to find out where to put a 50-cent pack of cotton balls (I eventually gave up). And customers were always asking where they could find particular toys. Where is Gumby? When will the Harry Potter merchandise arrive? Do you have any electric trains that make hooting noises? Where can I find the chess sets that were advertised for $1.99? Customers were impatient and assumed you were stupid if you didn't know and had to ask. And then there were the myriad tasks associated with selling merchandise, like finding the correct price when the tag was missing and it was the last one, or finding the original shipping carton for the $750 Barbie, or figuring out mailing charges, or dialing in credit card authorizations when the computers crashed.

After two weeks this knowledge became second nature, but those two weeks were very hard to endure. Every question or task had to be deferred; new workers depended on experienced ones to give them the necessary answers. This just added more work for them, another request in the queue, and it was not uncommon for them to feel harassed by new workers. Experienced workers sometimes avoided the newer ones—"Let them figure it out for themselves like I had to"—which added to the overall frustration of being new. Sometimes the new worker was reduced to begging for help because the problem wouldn't go away until the answer was found (or the shift was over). I once almost cried because no one would answer my page at the Toy Warehouse and the customers in line were getting impatient and surly. For those who survived the initiation period, this was a powerful incentive to stay on the job. No one wanted to start over. The cultural capital needed to work retail simply doesn't transfer from one store to another, even in the same chain. Everyone who is new starts at the bottom.

Another reason why it is hard to leave once expertise is acquired is that, ironically, workers come to feel *needed*. Although we all knew we were replaceable, there was a strong feeling that people depended on you to do your job. The schedule was organized in waves to promote this feeling: no one could take a break or have lunch until the person currently on break returned. Breaks are very precious to workers who are on their feet all day, so we monitored each other carefully to ensure that we could go on break when we were scheduled.[11] Mutual dependence was also evident when someone didn't show up to work, which immediately increased the stress level for everyone else, who had that many more transactions to accomplish. Quitting was hard, too, because who was going to answer all those questions if you weren't there? Solving problems and dealing with difficult situations all day builds in workers a sense of authority and a feeling of occupying a critical role in the overall division of labor. I agonized over quitting my jobs for this reason. I didn't want to let my coworkers down.

Every job enmeshes workers in social relationships, so it is not surprising that many come to feel as attached and committed to their jobs as I did (Cheever 2001). The importance of these ties is especially apparent in the case of the long-term workers. I jokingly referred to Dennis, one of my supervisors at Diamond Toys, as a "misanshop" because he constantly complained about the incivility of shoppers and the hopelessness of a career in retail. Knowing how much he hated his job—where he had worked for seven years—I was shocked the first time I saw him in the break room on his day off. He was waiting for a coworker to take his lunch break so they could go out together, and he had brought in his laptop computer to show others his new computer games. It was clear that his social life revolved around the store.

Many longtime workers developed quasi-familial bonds at the stores, referring to each other as brother and sister, mother and grandmother. This happened at both stores. There were also real kin networks, most evident at the Toy Warehouse. Some of the older employees brought their children or grandchildren with them to the store during their shift. These kids hung out in the break room or played with the demonstration toys, including the video games that were set up in the electronics department. All the employees helped to keep an eye on them. Those with older children sometimes got them jobs in the store.

I was an outsider to these family and friendship networks, but I was often very touched by the mutual support and caring I witnessed among my coworkers, especially at the Toy Warehouse. For the longtime workers, the store was an extension of their family networks and responsibilities. They used their employee discount cards (10 percent at the Toy Warehouse, 30 percent at Diamond Toys) to buy toys for their kin and quasi-kin. But more important was the social and emotional support they experienced there.

I was struck by this once when I was in the break room at the Toy Warehouse and my coworkers Dwain and Lamonica walked in on a day they were not scheduled to work. They were an African American couple in their early twenties who had been dating for a short time. They had come in to pick up their paychecks and to talk to Selma, an African American woman in her forties who had worked at the store for six years. Dwain was upset with his mother, who was giving him a very hard time, telling him he was worthless and criticizing him for being too dependent. During the discussion Lamonica was sitting on a stack of chairs behind Dwain, sucking on her Jamba Juice. She smiled during the conversation or rolled her eyes, as if to say, "What are you going to do?" But she didn't really participate. Selma, on the other hand, was giving him reassurance and sympathy and moral support. I asked her if she knew his mother and she said no, just what Dwain had told her. I realized that Selma was a mentor for Dwain; he clearly cherished her advice and encouragement.

This is the backstage of stores that most shoppers don't see, but it is critical for understanding why people stay in crummy jobs with low pay. Barbara Ehrenreich (2001) considers this conundrum in her study of low-wage work. She wonders why workers don't leave when other, higher-paying opportunities arise. At the Toy Warehouse, most workers stayed no longer than three months. Those who stayed long term did so because that was where their family was.

WHAT A DIFFERENCE A UNION MAKES

The union at Diamond Toys helped to ameliorate some of the most egregious problems with working retail. It guaranteed hours and schedules for senior associates, mandated longer rest breaks, and provided health benefits, vacation pay, and a career track. I earned 17 percent more at the unionized workplace, which was in line with the national 20 percent wage premium that comes with union membership (McCall 2001, 181). We were always allowed to leave when we were scheduled, whereas in the Toy Warehouse we were kept up to an hour later than scheduled to finish cleaning up the store after closing (a practice that routinely resulted in our being scheduled for fewer breaks than we were lawfully due). I was also impressed by how the managers behaved professionally and respectfully toward the workers. They quickly responded to pages and patiently explained procedures to the new people.

The unfortunate exception was *my* area manager, Dorothy. She rushed around our section barking orders and shouting insults at us. The first time I met her she told me that my name was unacceptable, as there were already two others in the store named Chris or Christine, so she was going to call me by my middle name instead. (Luckily that didn't last long because I couldn't remember to respond to Louise.) Sometimes when the store was busy she would stand next to me and shout, "Hurry, hurry, hurry." She would roll her eyes and mutter about my stupidity whenever I had to ask her a question or get her help to solve a problem. When I paged her she would pick up the phone and say in an exasperated voice, "What is it *now*, Christine?" It was some consolation that she treated everyone this way. We all found different ways to cope. Carl dealt with it by keeping a happy song in his head, he said. Alyss became depressed and frustrated; she often looked on the verge of tears. Dennis dreamed of leaving retail altogether and becoming a full-time teacher. Chandrika told me that to deal with the abuse she prayed. She also claimed to have filed four formal complaints against Dorothy, but nothing ever came of that. I fantasized about making a principled scene on my last day. (I didn't.)

This is the part of the job that a union can't change. Managers are allowed to harass workers, and there is virtually no recourse unless that harassment targets a worker's race, gender, or other legally protected characteristic (Williams 2003). The other managers and the store directors knew about Dorothy's abusive behavior but oddly seemed to tolerate it. They attributed it to personal and family problems she was experiencing. Rumors abounded about the nature of these problems, but it was impossible to verify them. I desperately wanted to understand why she was so mean, but in the end it probably wouldn't have made a difference. Sadistic bosses are an unfortunate fact of life in many hierarchical work organizations (Gherardi 1995).

The union offered no protection from harassing and abusive customers either. Admittedly this was a bigger problem at the Toy Warehouse than at Diamond Toys, but I don't think that customers were better behaved at Diamond Toys because of the union. For many customers, part of the allure of shopping at Diamond Toys was the educated and solicitous, not to mention white, sales staff. The mixture of class, race, and gender frames the customer-server relationship, just as it does the social organization of retail work. This is the subject of the next chapter.

CONCLUSION

Most sociological research on retail stores looks at them as sites of consumption. But stores are also workplaces. Retail work makes up an increasing proportion of the jobs in our economy. Yet these are "bad" jobs. According to Frank Levy (1998), a "good job" is one that pays enough to support a family and provides benefits, security, and autonomy. In contrast, most jobs in retail pay low wages, offer few benefits, have high turnover, and restrict workers' autonomy.

In this chapter, I have argued that the social organization of work in large toy stores also contributes to class, gender, and race inequalities. The Toy Warehouse, which had a predominately African American staff, paid extremely low wages, offered few benefits, and demanded "flexible" workers who made no scheduling demands. The store was segregated by race and gender, with white men in the director positions and African American women in managerial and supervisory roles. Among the staff, only white and light-skinned women and Asian American men were regularly assigned to cashiering positions, and only men (of all racial/ethnic groups) worked in the back room unloading and assembling the toys. African American men and women filled the positions of security guards, stockers, and gofers.

Because Diamond Toys was unionized, it offered better pay than the Toy Warehouse (but not a "living wage"), and its employees received health care and vacation benefits. Schedules were posted in advance, legally mandated breaks were honored, and career ladder promotions were available. For all of these reasons, a union does make a positive difference for workers.

But unions are not a panacea for all of the problems of retail

work. Historically, unions have not successfully redressed exclusionary hiring and promotion policies that favor whites over
racial/ethnic minorities and men over women; some even claim
that unions have made these problems worse (Lichtenstein 2002).
Thus Diamond Toys was even more firmly segregated than the
Toy Warehouse, as evidenced by the complete absence of black
men. The predominately white staff at Diamond Toys was headed
by white men in the director positions and mostly white men and
women in managerial, supervisory, and security roles. The white,
Latina/o, and Asian American clerks were divided up on the floor
by gender, with men selling mostly boys' toys and women selling
baby toys and girls' toys. In both stores, Latinas monopolized the
subcontracted cleaning roles. Thus, even though selling toys at
Diamond Toys was a better job than selling toys at the Toy
Warehouse, it was a highly segregated and exclusionary workplace. Even with a union, working at Diamond Toys would not
qualify as a "good job."

Debating the relative strengths and weaknesses of unionized
jobs may be moot, however. Union membership is at a hundred-
year low, hovering at around 9 percent of the private workforce
(Lichtenstein 2002). Regrettably, early in 2003 it was announced
that the Diamond Toys where I worked was closing, unable to
compete with the low prices of the nonunion discount chains. Retail giants have been extremely successful at preventing the formation of unions among their workers. High job turnover and
"right to work" laws make it easy for employers to fire anyone who
attempts to organize in the workplace. In the few instances where
organizing efforts have been successful, national retailers (including Kmart and Wal-Mart) have shown that they would rather shut
down franchises than recognize a union (Lichtenstein 2002).

On the other hand, conditions seemed favorable for organizing at the Toy Warehouse. Several of my coworkers expressed interest in employee organizing and spoke often of the importance of defending their rights. In fact, on my very first day of work at the Toy Warehouse I was lectured by a twenty-one-year-old security guard for not protecting my rights. This happened on my first eight-hour shift at the Toy Warehouse. It began with the three new people (me, Socorro, and Pak Chew) meeting in the break room. Here is an excerpt from my field notes from that day:

> We were sitting around the table with a couple of older men and Luther, who was African American and dressed in street clothes. He was the plainclothes security guard for the store, but I didn't know this at first. He was talking loudly and monopolizing the conversation. His topic was worker rights, and he was telling us about the importance of defending and supporting our rights. We were not in a union, so he said that we needed to take our complaints to the labor relations board and that there was one in every city. He gave us examples from his past of how he was able to use the labor relations board to fight for his rights, as in one case where an employer tried to fire him after eighty-nine days because at ninety days some benefits kicked in, and he said that the labor board helped him to get a $3,000 settlement. He said that if someone refused to hire you for a job like one at the Toy Warehouse, it was discrimination, and that you should tell the employer that, and if they didn't hire you, then take it to the board. He said anyone could get a job at the Toy Warehouse, it didn't require any skills, so if they didn't hire you and they had a sign that said "now hiring" you should kick up a fuss about it. Then he asked me what my job was here, and I said I was new so I didn't know yet, and he asked, but what job did

I apply for, and I said, "Anything." He told me that this was a big mistake because "anything" meant "everything" and the employer could get you by running you ragged and by saying you didn't do your job because you didn't have a job description. Socorro said she had applied for cashier and Pak Chew for electronics so they were considered in a more approving manner, but I had clearly messed up according to Luther. He said that was OK, that I had learned something today and he had taught something, so the day was a good one for him.

Luther was one of a number of workers at the Toy Warehouse who openly criticized management in the break room. Clearly, not everyone at the store supported collective action: recall that Michelle had a difficult time rallying enthusiasm for resisting unfair scheduling practices because many feared that they would lose their jobs if they complained. But there seemed to be a high degree of critical class consciousness at that store. My coworkers were aware that they had rights that were regularly violated by the Toy Warehouse, but they lacked any organized means of resistance.

Workers deserve better. But the growth of the service sector in our economy has resulted in an ever-diminishing proportion of "good jobs." This trend began nearly a generation ago, in the 1980s, when the transfer of manufacturing jobs from the United States to the third world inspired national concern. The North American Free Trade Agreement (NAFTA) was said to generate a "giant sucking sound" as good, industrial production jobs were swept south of the border into Mexico and Central America, leaving behind only poorly paid, unskilled service jobs in their wake. In the film *Roger and Me* (1989), Michael Moore documented this loss and its devastating impact on Flint, Michigan, as jobs in unionized auto manufacturing plants were replaced by marginal jobs selling Amway products, flipping burgers, and staffing burgeoning prisons. How could local communities like Flint, let alone the entire U.S. economy, be sustained on such bad, service sector jobs?

The short answer is, they can't. However, there is no reason why service sector jobs have to remain "bad" jobs. After all, manufacturing jobs did not start as "good" jobs. Anyone who has read Upton Sinclair, Charles Dickens, or the young Karl Marx is surely aware that factory labor was ill paid, dirty, and dangerous when it started. Factory jobs became good jobs only because, in the 1920s and 1930s, workers fought and bled for changes in policy and law. These jobs didn't become good jobs because of the magnanimity of factory owners. The motivations of the nineteenth-century robber barons were similar to those of the owners of Wal-Mart and other large retail outlets today: In the pursuit of profit, these owners of capital aimed to exploit labor to the extent permissible by law. Just as a great deal of organized effort was required to transform manufacturing jobs into good, sustainable jobs, the same is true of service jobs today. Later in this book, in chapter 6, I will discuss some of these efforts that are currently under way.

In addition to changing toy stores' economic organization, restructuring their jobs is necessary to alter their gender and race dynamics. As I have argued, the hierarchical and functional placement of workers according to managerial stereotypes results in advantages for white men and (to a lesser extent) white women and disadvantages for racial/ethnic minority men and women. These stereotypes are perhaps more deeply entrenched than low wages, based as they are on perceptions of customer preferences.

Consumers therefore have a role in pressing for changes in these job assignments. But in my view, the struggle for equal access to "bad jobs" is hardly worth an organized effort. There is little point in demanding equal access to jobs that don't support a family. Similarly, career ladders have to be created before equal opportunities for advancement are demanded. The fight against racism and sexism, then, should be folded into efforts to economically upgrade these jobs. The goal of restructuring jobs in toy stores, and in retail work in general, should be self-sufficiency—and hope—for all workers, regardless of race or gender.

4

INEQUALITY ON THE SHOPPING FLOOR

Erving Goffman (1967), the master of sociological observation, claimed that face-to-face public encounters with strangers typically rely on ritualized scripts to make them go smoothly. In service work, this insight has been transformed into a maxim. Visit any fast-food restaurant, big box retailer, or major theme park, and you are likely to experience a rigid set of normative assumptions and expectations about how to comport yourself. At McDonald's, for example, you are likely to encounter the "six steps of counter service" (Leidner 1993), beginning with the question "May I take your order please?" and, until recently, "Do you want to supersize that?" Usually, this scripted server-customer interaction comes off without a hitch. When it doesn't, the result is often conflict. If customers linger too long over their food order, or request some special item not on the menu, they will likely face opprobrium, mostly from the customers behind them in line. Workers who refuse to say their lines will likely be fired.

There are both pros and cons to highly ritualized service work. On the one hand, the routinized scripts ensure predictability and efficiency for customers and offer some protection for the privacy and personal identity of the workers. Their major drawback is their tendency to dehumanize social encounters. Workers are treated like robots, without feelings or needs; rarely do they even achieve recognition for their labor.

Some sociologists have unwittingly contributed to this dehumanization of retail workers. George Ritzer (1999), for example, calls them "simulated people" who are "all playing well defined roles":

> Their employing organizations have developed a series of guidelines about how they are supposed to look, speak, behave, and so forth. The result is that these positions can be filled by a wide range of individuals. There is little or no room for creativity or individuality. It could be argued that . . . the counterpersons are simulations—they are fakes. . . . Instead of "real" human interaction with servers in fast food restaurants, with clerks in shopping malls and superstores, with telemarketers, and so on, we can think of these as simulated interactions. . . . Authentic interaction rarely if ever takes place. (116–17)

In Ritzer's view, ritualized service interactions are, by their very nature, dehumanized encounters. When salesclerks follow a script, they seem robotic—not fully human—and thus not deserving of dignity and respect.

This image of the service worker as a "simulation," is, of course, the customer's perspective. What happens when we shift focus and look at the customer-server interaction from the worker's perspective? We realize that ritualized service work, like acting, requires a great deal of physical effort, emotional stamina, and self-control. Katherine Newman (1999), who studied fast-food restaurants from the perspective of workers, recognized that finesse, patience, and forbearance are required to succeed in these jobs. She writes, "We can think of these jobs as lowly, repetitive, routinized, and demeaning, or we can recognize that doing them right requires their incumbents to process information, coordinate with others, and track inventory. These valuable competencies are tucked away inside jobs that are popularly characterized as utterly lacking in skill" (144). As a former salesclerk, I can attest that only the most skilled worker can make the service interaction appear automatic, unthinking, and routine.

Shifting the vantage point to workers also reveals that these ritualized jobs are not (and perhaps cannot) be filled by a wide range of individuals. As we saw in the previous chapter, service workers are not entirely interchangeable, since race and gender are built into the job requirements. For instance, black men were not hired at Diamond Toys, and the few men who were regularly assigned the duty of cashiering at the Toy Warehouse were Asian American. Because managers imagine different kinds of people for different jobs, and because many employees develop a personal, psychological stake in that division, only limited crossovers in job assignments occur.

In this chapter, I explore the consequences of this job sorting for interactions between clerks and customers. I argue that race and gender segregation of jobs perpetuates stereotypes that shape the meanings and consequences of routinized shopping encounters. When different kinds of people fill each role in a ritualized service encounter, the result is the reproduction of social inequality.

To illustrate this, imagine a service industry where all servers would be women and all customers men. This was the scenario encountered by Arlie Hochschild (1983) in her study of flight at-

tendants in the 1970s. She argued that this stratification reinforced assumptions linking femininity with servility and masculinity with economic and social power. As Goffman (1977) observes, virtually any stereotype will come to seem natural and
inevitable if ritualized interactions that reinforce it are repeated
often enough (see also West and Zimmerman 1987). Because the
sorting of people into jobs on the basis of not only gender but also
race is very common in our economy, service work has become a
major source of group stereotypes and prejudices.

Of course, in actual practice, service rituals are often modified.
Despite their goal of precisely scripting the service encounter,
corporations cannot control all interactions between clerks and
customers. Contrary to Ritzer's impression, there is always room
for creativity and individual expression within the constraints of
the role. Corporate ideals have to be translated into local contexts. In a study of Burger King and McDonald's restaurants in
New York City, Jennifer Parker Talwar (2002) found that the
scripts mandated by these companies had to be changed according to the ethnic makeup of the neighborhoods where the restaurants were located. For instance, the requirement that workers always smile upset many customers in a predominately Chinese
neighborhood, who interpreted the behavior as overly pushy. In
one franchise, greeters were hired to welcome customers respectfully at the front door and accompany them to the order
counter to assist them in making their selections.

Not only local context but the actual mix of customer and clerk
will shape the service encounter. In this chapter, I describe how
white service workers encounter a different set of customer expectations than black service workers, resulting in different mod-

ifications of the scripted role. Likewise, white customers encounter a different set of service worker expectations than black
customers.

Patricia Hill Collins (2000) uses the concept of a "matrix of
domination" to analyze these shifting configurations of race and
gender and their consequences for social interaction. In contrast
to those who might assume that all women face similar forms of
domination and oppression, she argues that sexism comes in a variety of forms that are shaped by the contexts of race, social class,
and sexuality. Discrimination against black women is different
from discrimination against white women because these groups
are located at different places on what she calls the matrix of domination. Black women are typically subject to domination on the
basis of gender, race, and class, while white women suffer from
gender domination but are privileged by their race and often by
their class as well. This matrix operates at all levels of society and
culture. Its workings are evident in the scarcity of black women
and the total absence of black men at the higher-paying Diamond
Toys compared to their overrepresentation at the Toy Warehouse. It is also apparent in the division of tasks within the stores,
where white men monopolize the director positions, white or
light-skinned women are concentrated in cashiering jobs, and
darker-skinned African American women and men work as stockers and gofers.

In this chapter I explore how the matrix of domination shapes,
but does not fully determine, customer-worker interactions in the
toy store. I focus on the interaction rules that govern the shopping floor and how they reproduce stereotypes about different
groups. There are both formal rules, developed by corporations,
and informal rules, developed by workers to protect their dignity

and self-respect. I also discuss what happens when these rules are not followed and interactions break down into conflict. Whether the interaction can be repaired will depend on the matrix because different groups have different resources to draw on to assert their will in the toy store. It will also depend on the creativity and personalities of the individuals involved. The meanings of workplace rituals are not fixed and self-evident but change depending on the mix of individuals engaged in the interaction. Only through a process of symbolic interaction among active, creative, knowledgeable participants do the meanings and consequences of these rituals emerge (Blumer 1969).

Before discussing interactions on the shopping floor, however, I describe the normative expectations of the customer-clerk relationship. Corporations set the stage for the interactions that happen within the store by scripting ideal performances. These ideals are generated by corporate boards whose imaginings may bear little resemblance to the actual circumstances of store life, but they nevertheless form a backdrop to daily practice. They shape employee training regimes, hiring policies, and customers' expectations of what kind of experience awaits them in the store. Some workers recognize themselves in these company imaginings, and they seek out these jobs and robustly perform their roles. Others are more cynical and resistant, but they are still constrained by the rules of the corporation that limit how service workers may interact with customers.

CORPORATE CULTURE IN TOY STORES

Stores go to a lot of trouble to distinguish themselves from one another by developing distinctive themed environments. Since nearly every store in a specialty area offers the same goods, specialty retailers attempting to capture market share focus on developing innovations in store layout, decorations, and services. Their goal is to entertain as they sell. Thus toy stores, like other specialty stores, now sell a "mood" in addition to Barbies and Big Wheels.

The Toy Warehouse and Diamond Toys represented different moods that were intended to appeal to different desires, if not different sectors, of the toy-buying public. Both stores were parts of international chains of toy stores. The stores were governed by central corporate headquarters on the East Coast and regional offices located throughout the country. Corporate boards imagined what the store was supposed to look like, what kind of person shopped at the store, and how employees were supposed to behave. Advertising campaigns instructed consumers on this corporate culture. Employees learned about it in employee handbooks, videos, posters in the employee break room, and specific instructions handed down the chain of command from store director to manager to supervisor to salesclerk.

The corporation that owned the Toy Warehouse wanted its stores to create a fun, family-oriented atmosphere filled with discovery and delight. Sales workers were expected to demonstrate a high degree of spirited enthusiasm. We were required to hand out balloons and stickers to children and sing to them on their birthdays. The name badge I wore proclaimed that I had been "delighting guests since 2001." Like all new employees, I was required on my first morning shift to hula-hoop in front of the staff, presumably to set the stage for the fun career ahead of me. All of us clerks were required to form a gauntlet around the front door when the store opened and applaud the customers as they entered the store (there were always people waiting to enter the store in the morning), much to their bewilderment.

Corporate culture is usually communicated to new hires through perfunctory training sessions that last no more than one day. At the Toy Warehouse, our training consisted of watching nine twenty-minute videotapes on everything from handling returns to selling the new Game Boy. Some of the videos had no point other than to inspire and excite us as new members of the Toy Warehouse team. One, entitled *Magic Moment*, was filmed during a corporate convention in 1999. The video showed the vice presidents of the various divisions of "The Warehouse" gathered on a stage. Each said a little bit about his division, to roaring applause from the audience. The audience was made up of store directors and managers from around the country. All of the corporate heads on stage were middle-aged white men wearing polo shirts and khaki pants; slightly more diversity was evident in the audience. Then the CFO was introduced (he was Asian American). He announced three major corporate changes. First, from now on customers would be referred to as "guests." "What will they be called now?" he asked the audience, and the audience shouted, "*Guests!*" "I can't hear you!" "*Guests!*" Second, from now on the main corporate offices would be referred to as "store support centers." Third (there was a drum roll), there would be a 10 percent employee discount! At this the crowd went wild. Then there was a bizarre segue to an orchestra leading the gathered managers in a xylophone song. Socorro, one of the two other new hires watching the videos with me, mercifully took it upon herself to fast-forward through this.

While we were suffering through the videos, very loud conversations were taking place in the employee break room next door. I couldn't see who was in there, but I could hear them because the door between the two rooms was open. The employees in the break room were yelling and swearing about all sorts of things, from relationships to money. This was a little off-putting to me, but my fellow new hires didn't seem at all affected. There seemed to be a lot of discontent and rabble-rousing. Someone (whom I later found out was Michelle) said that she had been given a raise of only 25 cents and that the manager could shove it up her ass. Every once in a while someone poked his or her head into our room, I think because there was a phone in there that he or she wanted to use, or the person wanted to drop off more junk in this catastrophically messy room. One heavily tattooed white man with earrings peered in at us watching the videos and looked disgusted, as if it was meaningless propaganda.

Clearly, the corporation didn't imagine any of this.

While the Toy Warehouse aspired to present an image as an exciting playground for kids and their families, Diamond Toys portrayed itself as a high-end specialty store oriented toward meeting the needs of discriminating adult shoppers. The store aimed to flatter the sophisticated tastes of the elite. The very setup of the store encouraged this aura. Diamond Toys looked like a fancy department store, not like a warehouse. A uniformed doorman out front greeted customers. Inside there were lavish displays of giant toys with mechanical moving parts. A theme song played in a continuous loop, making me at times feel trapped inside a ride at Disneyland. The store also seemed to have the theme park effect on the many adults and children who stood in awe and marveled at the displays.

The effectiveness of corporate advertising on some adults was astounding. On one occasion, a white male shopper approached one of my coworkers and asked to be shown to the "special" room reserved for the best customers. He asserted that this special room was filled with the most expensive and exclusive toys that were not on display for the general public. My coworker tried to convince him that no such room existed, but he insisted. He said that a friend had shared with him the secret password that allowed admission to the special room but that he had forgotten it. My coworker's insistence that this was simply a myth only bolstered his conviction that the special room existed.

We didn't have to watch videos during our training at Diamond Toys. Instead we were issued an employee handbook. The personnel manager, Leslie, took the three new hires to a seminar room and read the entire thirty-page document to us. We were invited to interrupt the presentation at any time to ask questions.

Much was said about the dress code. We were required to wear the company-issued maroon polo shirt tucked into belted chino slacks or skirt. Belts had to be black, tan, cordovan, or brown. No outside stitching or pockets were allowed, as this conveyed the look of jeans, which were forbidden. Leslie showed us where the ironing board and iron were kept "just in case" we needed them. We were allowed only two earrings per ear and a single nose stud. No visible tattoos, and no unconventional hair color.

The corporate instruction we received as salesclerks was summed up in the "Five I's of Customer Service." These were Initiate, Inquire, Inform, Include, and Into the Register. We were told that we had to initiate contact within thirty seconds with each customer who wandered into our section. The corporation offered some suggestions on the best ways to do this: we might invite them to play with a toy, comment on some article of their clothing ("That's a great Bulls sweatshirt!"), or mention some little-known fact about the merchandise ("Did you realize that that $99 stuffed animal is 100 percent washable?"). Leslie admitted that these were ridiculous and encouraged us to improvise our lines. After a successful initiation, we were instructed to inquire about the customer's needs with open-ended questions or remarks, like "Tell me about the kind of party you are planning." At the "inform" stage we were to match the customer's needs with product features (which we never got instruction about), and at the "include" stage we were to recommend accessories to complement the main purchase (such as doll clothes for dolls). Our goal was to sell a minimum of two UPTs, or units per transaction. We received a printout three times per shift showing us how we were doing.

Each step of the selling system was designed to convey the clerk's expertise and solicitous interest in meeting the customer's every need and desire. When we were on the floor and not serving customers, we were expected to stand in the aisles (not behind the counter) and wait for a customer to arrive. No hands in pockets (I was reprimanded for doing that once). No talking with other employees. No leaving the section. We were required to straighten the toy displays in our areas, but we didn't do any restocking. We were there to serve.

Thus the corporate board of Diamond Toys imagined a sales staff of Jeeves-like butlers. Correspondingly, their ideal customer was a member of the bourgeoisie in need of professional consultation on their purchases. Oddly, this customer was never shown in the instructional materials. There weren't any people in the toy catalogs, either; the focus was always on the "special" merchandise we offered.

The Toy Warehouse, on the other hand, was quite explicit

about what its ideal customer looked like: she was a middle-class, white mother. Several of the videos that we were required to watch featured this woman and demonstrated the ways we were supposed to serve her. She usually knew what she wanted (a Game Boy, for instance), but she might need to be told that it required game cartridges, batteries, and a light worm. She didn't like to be kept waiting, so we were supposed to work quickly to accommodate her (no lingering over party decorations). My manager, Olive, urged me to treat every woman in the store as if she were my mother. Mothers made the purchasing decisions, she said, so they got the special treatment. Olive (who listened to motivational tapes from the corporate office during her two-hour commute each way to work) said that the average child has $20,000 spent on toys for him or her before he or she was eighteen, and the Toy Warehouse wanted to be the place where most of that money is spent.

Advertising and other forms of propaganda displayed in the Toy Warehouse were directed to middle-class families. The store "sponsored" National Day for Children, for example, which was celebrated by posting signs that read "National Day for Children" and putting out a stack of leaflets on a card table that gave "10 reasons to celebrate your child!" But nothing actually happened in the store. As far as I could tell, the National Day for Children was endorsed by the corporate office for the sole purpose of making the store seem dedicated to the best interests of children and families. Also offered were a college savings plan (which put a small percentage of any purchase in a special account for college tuition), a parenting newsletter, and a summer camp program where children could be dropped off for a two-hour activity on weekday mornings.

In the six weeks that I worked at the store I never saw anyone take advantage of these corporate initiatives. The summer camp was especially interesting to me. Two employees staffed the "camp," which consisted of a few card tables with a tablecloth set up in the store. Activities were barely disguised promotional gimmicks, like a "Play Doh factory" day or a Pokemon word search game (where kids searched for the names of the Pokemon characters in a word search puzzle). Only parents who didn't work during the day and who had their own transportation could take advantage of this program. But middle-class housewives would not bring their kids to the store and leave them there, and poor parents wouldn't have felt welcomed or, if they did, would not have the time or necessary transportation to bring their children in. Not surprisingly, then, the only children I ever saw participating in the program were the children of employees.

The child imagined by the Toy Warehouse's corporate office was thus middle class and college bound, from a traditional family where Mom didn't work for pay but did all the shopping. Children were imagined as consumers but not buyers; that was the mother's role. Children were expected to have their own ideas about what they wanted. The store sold gift cards to give to children for their birthdays and special occasions. These were little plastic cards that looked like credit cards. They were packaged in greeting card envelopes with a space to write in the child's name and the dollar amount of the gift.

Children were much less central to the marketing agenda of Diamond Toys. Although they were the ultimate consumers of most of the merchandise, they were treated more like pampered and coddled pets than willing and agentic buyers. Adults were our primary focus; it was to them that we directed our "expert" knowledge and solicitous attention. Leslie told us that people came to our store and were willing to pay more because we were "the ultimate toy experts." (In contrast, the Toy Warehouse considered kids the ultimate toy experts.) At Diamond Toys, we did not strive to make the shopping experience fun for families; rather, the mood we aspired to set was one of careful and quiet deliberation to assist adults in making a suitable, if not ideal, purchase.

How did these corporate expectations play out in practice? In the most obvious sense, they selected for different kinds of customers. As I've noted, shoppers at the Toy Warehouse represented all levels of our stratified society, while Diamond Toys attracted a more upper-class clientele. Furthermore, the Toy Warehouse seemed more child dominated, whereas adults controlled most purchases at Diamond Toys. I'll discuss children and their relationships in the stores in the next chapter. In the remainder of this chapter I will describe the impact of the corporate culture on customer-worker interactions on the shopping floor. Retail workers were expected to conform to the corporate culture, but they often developed their own rules for dealing with customers that clashed with that agenda. These informal rules were more flexible than the corporate ones. Also unlike the corporate ones, they more explicitly took into account the matrix of domination.

SHOP-FLOOR CULTURE

Interactions between customers and workers in toy stores are governed by informal rules that are shaped but not determined by the corporate cultures. These rules are sometimes known as "the ropes." New hires pick up the ropes from observing experienced workers.

One of the first lessons I learned on the shopping floor was that middle-class white women shoppers got whatever they wanted. I suppose that as a middle-class white woman I should have found this empowering. Instead I came to understand it as a result of race and class privilege.

Most of the customers at both stores were women. At the Toy Warehouse we were told that women made 90 percent of the purchase decisions, so we were to treat women deferentially. Olive told me that the store abided by the "$19,800 rule." If a customer wanted to return merchandise and it was questionable whether we should take the return (because it had been broken or worn out by the customer, or because the customer had lost the receipt), we should err on the side of the customer. A $200 loss today might please the customer so much that she would return to the store and spend the rest of the $20,000 on each of her children.

But in my experience only the white women got this kind of treatment. Not surprisingly, many developed a sense of entitlement and threw fits when they were not accommodated. The following example from my field notes is from the Toy Warehouse.

> A white woman in her fifties came into the store to pick up a bike that she had ordered two days previously. She had paid for the bike to be assembled and ready for her to pick up that day. She waited for almost a half hour as we scoured the back room for the bike. We couldn't find it. The woman was getting madder and madder as she waited. There were some other bikes like it that were in boxes and the bike guys of-

fered to assemble one for her, but that would have required another wait, so she yelled, "To hell with it, give me my money back, and I will never ever come to this store again!" She demanded to talk to the manager. Olive tried to appease her by offering her a $25 gift certificate, but she refused and yelled about how terrible we all were. After she left the store Olive called the whole staff up to the service desk and chewed us out. Losing this customer was a really big deal to Olive.

Afterwards, the workers talked about this woman. One said that her face looked like the face of someone who was almost always angry and abusive. Everyone agreed that she came into the store in a bad mood, wanting to pick a fight. Furthermore, the store's promise to her, to have her bike ready for pickup in two days, was unreasonable given the understaffing of the store. Should workers earning $7.50 an hour shoulder the blame for not meeting the expectations of a middle-class consumer? We didn't think so. Besides, $25 seemed like a good deal for her troubles compared to our meager rewards. This shopper didn't realize that the low price she paid for her bike was the result of underpaying us, the salesclerks. We were in effect subsidizing her purchase. It shouldn't have been a mystery why we shrugged off her minor inconvenience.

Many middle-class shoppers freely complained to me about the store, assuming that I cared about their satisfaction with their shopping experience. (Frankly, I thought it would be a better job without them.) They seemed to consider their feedback a form of valuable advice that the company could use to develop a better store. These shoppers either thought I was a manager or expected me to be a conduit to management. But neither store where I worked ever solicited my advice. Workers could no more easily communicate a customer's opinion than we could our own. Our almost complete lack of power and influence over store operations was a perfect counterpoint to the sense of efficacy and self-importance conveyed to us by middle-class customers.

Middle-class white women had a reputation at the store of being especially demanding and abusive toward salesclerks. Susan, a thirty-five-year-old Latina, agreed with my observation that rich white women were the most demanding customers; she said they always demanded to see the manager and always got appeased. Susan, one of the people who taught me the ropes at the service desk, said that Latinas/os never demanded to see the manager and never threatened to stop shopping at the Toy Warehouse. I asked if she had ever seen a black person do this; at first she said no, and then she said yes. She remembered that sometimes at the end of the month poor blacks got upset at the service desk and demanded to see a manager. She explained that at the end of the month if they ran out of money they might try to return the merchandise that they had purchased earlier in the month but that had already been used. If the workers at the service desk turned down the request for a refund, they demanded to see the manager. But, she said, they were not going to get satisfaction. Susan claimed that the store only cared about what the rich white women thought because they were the ones chosen to respond to the customer service surveys.

The surveys that Susan was referring to were conducted by the corporate office. It is unlikely that race and gender were used to choose respondents, as Susan suggested they were. Cashiers were required to ask all customers for their addresses and phone numbers to be on our catalog list; this was also how the store compiled the names used for the survey. Every other week, eight individuals from the list were called at random and asked about their shopping experience at the Toy Warehouse. It is possible that middle-class white women made up most of the respondents if this group was most likely to respond to a telephone inquiry, but we did not record any demographic information in the database.

This survey was the source of our notoriously low customer satisfaction rating, reputedly the lowest in the region. The results of the biweekly survey were posted in the employee break room. During the time I worked there, we never reached the "acceptable" score of 78 (out of 100 possible), despite the director's promise to buy pizza for everyone if we ever achieved that goal. A sign on the wall of the break room said "78 puts pizza on the plate!" The best we ever did while I was there was 48.

Susan's remarks about demanding and complaining shoppers illustrate some of the elaborate stereotypes that service desk workers used in the course of their daily transactions. Immediate assumptions were made about customers based on their race, gender, and apparent social class; workers responded to customers using these cues.

Because middle-class white women were the most coveted customers at the Toy Warehouse, many developed a sense of entitlement. On one occasion, a very pregnant white woman came up to the service desk to return a teddy bear mobile for over the baby crib. The mechanism that played music and moved the mobile wasn't working, so she wanted to exchange it for one that was working. We sent her into the store to find another one for an even exchange. She came back after quite a while with another one in a box that she had opened. (Customers weren't supposed to open the factory-sealed boxes, but we didn't say anything.) She said that one package that she had opened also had a broken mechanism but that she had found a mobile with a different motif (clowns instead of teddy bears) made by the same company that had a mechanism in it that worked. She asked if she could replace that for the broken one in her original box. She said, "So will you do this and make a customer happy? If you do it I will come back to shop here more, and if you don't I won't ever set foot in the store. So what's it going to be? Do you want a happy customer or not?" I couldn't believe the attitude but I kept my mouth shut. I thought about the floor workers who would get in trouble for all those open boxes. My supervisor Vannie said she could make the switch. The woman never said thank you, but then customers rarely did.

To me, one of the most eye-opening examples of white women's sense of entitlement that I witnessed in the Toy Warehouse was their refusal to check their bags at the counter. Since stealing was such a big problem in the store, customers were required to leave all large bags and backpacks at the service desk. A large sign indicating this policy was posted on the store's entrance. The vast majority of customers carrying bags immediately approached the desk to comply with the rule. The exception was white women, who almost universally ignored the sign. When challenged, they would argue—"But my wallet is in there!" or "I need my bag with me!"—and we would have to insist so as not to appear unfair to the other people. I guiltily recognized myself in their behavior. Since then, I have always turned over my bag.

White women developed a sense of entitlement because in most instances they got what they wanted. Members of other groups who wanted to return used merchandise, or who needed special consideration, were rarely granted their requests. The week before the bike incident I was on a register that broke down in the middle of a credit card transaction. A middle-class black woman in her forties was buying in-line skates for her ten-year-old daughter. The receipt came out of the register but not the slip for her to sign, so I had to call a manager. Olive came over and explained that she needed to go to another register and repeat the transaction, but the customer said no way, since it had seemed to go through all right and she didn't want to be charged twice. She had to wait over an hour to get this situation resolved, and she wasn't offered any compensation. She didn't yell or make a scene; she acted stoically through the long wait for a resolution. I felt bad for her. I went over to the service desk to tell a couple of my fellow workers there what was happening while the managers tried to resolve it, and I said they should just give her the skates and let her go. My fellow workers thought that was the funniest thing they had ever heard. I said, "What about Olive's $19,800 rule about letting things go to make sure we keep loyal customers?" but they just laughed at me. Celeste said, "I want Christine to be the manager, she just lets the customers have whatever they want!"

It has been well documented that African Americans suffer discrimination in public places, including stores (Feagin and Sikes 1995); this phenomenon is sometimes referred to jokingly as "shopping while black" (Williams 2004). They report being followed by security, treated harshly by attendants, and flatly refused service. The flip side of this discrimination is the privilege experienced by middle-class whites. This privilege is not recognized precisely because it is so customary. Whites expect first-rate service; when it is not forthcoming, some feel victimized, even discriminated against. This was especially apparent in the Toy

Warehouse, where most of the salespeople were black. I noticed that when white women customers were subjected to long waits in line, or if they received what they perceived as uncaring attention, they would often sigh loudly, roll their eyes, and try to make eye contact with other whites, looking for a sign of recognition that the service they were receiving was inferior and unfair.

I played into this behavior on several occasions, especially early on when I was learning the ropes. A white customer was holding up the return line because she was upset that her "half-price coupon" for Barbies didn't apply to the one she had selected, a Barbie dressed up as Dorothy from the *Wizard of Oz*. She was arguing about this with two of my coworkers, who were both black, and trying to get me involved in the discussion. She asked me pointedly to look at the coupon and say whether it explicitly excluded the one she wanted. I said "Apparently not," and that just fueled her fire. The store director was called, a white man about my age, and the argument moved to another register. Eventually, he agreed to sell her the doll for half-price, even though the discount technically didn't apply. One of my co-workers who was following this came back to me afterwards and said I could get into trouble for agreeing with customers. I was shocked! She told me that in the argument with the director, the customer had said, "But Christine said the coupon applied!" She knew my name because I wore a name tag. She had used racial privilege and racial solidarity to get what she wanted.

This customer had assumed erroneously that I had more authority than the others because I was white. Just as white customers are treated with more respect, so are white service workers, especially by white customers. Judith Rollins (1985, 129), who studied domestic workers, writes that whites often prefer to

employ whites for child care because they see whites as "more refined, articulate, potentially upwardly mobile, and intelligent"
than nonwhites. At the Toy Warehouse, where I was one of only
four white women workers, I noticed that shoppers frequently assumed that I was in charge.

This assumption was especially clear on one occasion at the
Toy Warehouse, when I was being trained at the service desk.
There was a group of three customers in line at one time as Tanesha, a twenty-three-year-old African American woman, was training me. The first person in line was an Indian woman who returned an item and was given her refund on a merchandise credit
card. She already had a card from a previous exchange and she
wanted to combine the amounts of the two cards onto one card.
Tanesha thought she knew how to do this, so she tried, but it got
all tangled up in the computer system and she had to call for
backup help from Olive. This upset the other customers in line.
I was kind of mad at the woman for asking for the two cards to be
made into one since there were people waiting and what was the
big deal having two cards anyway? When she asked for this I suggested to her that it was going to take some time to figure it out
and she said that was OK, she would wait. Then when it got complicated (after maybe five minutes) she said that she would just
take the two cards back, but by then it was too late, she didn't have
that option. While Tanesha was trying to figure out how to work
the system, the other customers in line (two white women) were
getting irritated. They elbowed up to the counter and complained to me about the wait. I said something about being in
training, and they thought I meant that I was training Tanesha.
So they said, "Well, call up someone else to the register!" I said
I'd have to ask Tanesha to do this. They demanded that I stop

training Tanesha for a moment to call another person to the exchange desk. I said, "No you don't understand, I'm the one who is in training, she knows what she is doing and she is the only one who can call for backup and she is in the middle of trying to accommodate this other customer." I think they were embarrassed by their presumption that the white woman was in charge. When they figured out their mistake they looked mortified and stepped back from the counter.

In addition to assuming that I was in charge, customers at both stores frequently assumed that I was an expert on childhood. This was not an altogether irrational assumption, since I was working in a toy store and shoppers frequently ask clerks for advice about the merchandise they sell. I suppose that some might assume that I looked like a mother with personal experience of children's toys. But I didn't have children, and I knew virtually nothing about toys or children's popular culture before I took these jobs. And I wasn't alone in this. Consumers should realize that workers being paid $7 to $8 per hour do not have any expertise about the merchandise they are selling—whether that's toys, clothing, electronics, or anything else. We received no training whatsoever. Any advice we gave we literally made up.

At the Toy Warehouse, customers didn't expect elaborate advice from the salesclerks. Those who stopped me in the aisles asked me simple questions, like where to find particular toys, or to help them find out the price for items with missing price tags. I also fielded many questions about the suitability of toys for certain age groups. For example, one woman wanted to know if she should buy her four-year-old a Turbo Speller, even though the box clearly stated "6 and older." She wanted my reassurance that this didn't apply to her child.[1] Another wanted to know which

Game Boy games were appropriate for five-year-old children. But for the most part, customers realized that they were on their own in the store.

Anyone who has ever shopped in a big box store has probably observed workers trying to avoid customers, as if playing a game of hide-and-seek. Customers have to make a special effort to find a clerk if they need assistance. Customers search the aisles for a worker who seems to be trying to evade them. Crossing the floor, I would often look down to avoid eye contact with customers either because I was dealing with a previous request or because I was trying to make it to the break room for my fifteen-minute rest. The break room was at the far back end of the store, yet our break started when we left the registers at the front of the store. This was the case at both stores. If we were waylaid, the time we spent dealing with the customer was deducted from our fifteen-minute break.

Sometimes worker resistance to the unceasing demands of customers at the Toy Warehouse was more blatant. In addition to avoidance, we would sometimes perform our role halfheartedly, tell a customer we didn't carry a particular toy (even if we did), or palm off a demanding customer on a new or especially eager employee. In the break room we constantly made fun of customers' stupidity and congratulated each other on our ability to control disgusting and hostile shoppers. We also made an art out of ignoring requests. Next time you are in a large store, notice the intercom pages: workers are constantly being paged to respond to phone calls, customer requests, and problems that arise at the registers. At the Toy Warehouse these pages were ignored most of the time, which is one of the reasons why they were so ubiquitous. Once at the Toy Warehouse a customer asked the service desk worker to show him where the Superballs were displayed. This was a task for a merchandiser, who was paged to come to the service desk. After two additional, increasingly urgent pages from the service desk worker, Gail finally appeared, furious about having been forced to leave the break room. Because of perennial understaffing at the store, she responded to the page even though she was officially on break, but she wasn't happy about it. I watched the visibly shaken customer follow her as she stomped back into the aisles toward the Superballs, unleashing a loud, vitriolic commentary on the store's unfair labor practices.

In contrast, talking back or ignoring customers was taboo at Diamond Toys. Although we complained about and made fun of customers in the break room, we never expressed our disdain publicly. At Diamond Toys, catering to customers was our raison d'etre. It was not unusual to spend fifteen to twenty minutes dealing with a single customer. Customers frequently asked questions like "What are going to be the hot toys for one-year-olds this Christmas?" or "What one item would you recommend for two sisters of different ages?" One mother asked me to help her pick out a $58 quartz watch for her seven-year-old son. A personal shopper phoned in and asked me to describe the three Britney Spears dolls we carried, help her pick out the "nicest" one, and then arrange to ship it to her employer's niece. Customers also asked detailed questions about how the toys were meant to work and were especially curious about comparing the merits of the various educational toys we offered (for example, I was asked to compare the relative merits of the "Baby Mozart" and the "Baby Bach"). On my very first day on the floor, I answered a phone call from a customer who asked me to pick out toys for a one-year-old girl and a two-and-a-half-year-old boy, to spend up to $100, and to arrange to have the toys gift wrapped and mailed to their recipients.

At Diamond Toys most customers didn't mind waiting for their turn to consult with me. When the lines were long they didn't make rude huffing noises or try to make eye contact with their fellow sufferers. The two stores were staffed and structured quite differently, and that certainly helps to explain some differences in the experiences (and satisfaction) of the customers. We were so understaffed at the Toy Warehouse that I felt as if I were running the whole time I was at work. However, I couldn't help thinking that customers—who were mostly white—cut us more slack at Diamond Toys because most of us were white. We were presumed to be professional, caring, and knowledgeable even when we weren't. My African American coworkers at the Toy Warehouse, in contrast, were assumed to be incompetent and uncaring. Like the people who employed domestic workers studied by Julia Wrigley (1995), white customers seemed less respectful of racial/ethnic minority service workers than white workers; they were willing to pay more and wait more for the services of whites because they assumed that whites were more refined and intelligent.

The culture of the stores also reflected these race and class dynamics. Diamond Toys embodied whiteness both physically and symbolically, while the Toy Warehouse embodied a more diverse, creative, and flamboyant style. This was reflected in our uniforms, in the pace of the work, and in the general tone of conversation. The dress code was strictly enforced at Diamond Toys, much to the chagrin of my younger coworkers, who especially hated the belted and tucked-in look. Some tried to subvert it by wearing their pants low on their hips, but this was a minor alteration. I thought the uniforms were hideous. I was completely taken aback once when a customer complimented me on how I looked. I was on a ladder retrieving a doll stroller from the valence and a middle-aged white woman looked up, smiling, and said, "Your uniforms look so nice and comfortable!"

The dress code at Diamond Toys was not unlike the uniforms that many area school districts recently had imposed on elementary and middle school children, which probably explains my younger coworkers' disdain for them. But why did customers like them? Edward Morris (2005), who has written about school uniforms in minority schools, argues that a "tucked in shirt" signifies whiteness, middle-class respectability, and a professional demeanor, especially for the middle-class teachers who enforce the school dress code. (To the kids, in contrast, the uniforms evoked prison garb comparisons.) This analysis matches my experience at Diamond Toys, where our uniforms seemed to reassure customers that we were professionals who knew what we were talking about.

At the Toy Warehouse we wore company-issued bright orange vests over matching camp shirts, giving us the look of warehouse attendants. The bright colors were no doubt intended to make us easy to spot on the floor. We were allowed to wear black jeans to work. Most of the young men wore fashionable low riders that hung below their underwear and dragged on the floor. The young women wore super-skintight hip huggers. Since it was summer, we were also given the choice to wear shorts. Socorro told me that she wasn't planning to take advantage of that because people didn't need to see the tattoos on her calves. Most of my other coworkers were only too eager to show off their art, as they called it. The younger ones had multiple piercings, including tongue studs. Careful attention was also paid to hairstyles, the more outrageous and intricate, the better. Most men and women wore very elaborate hair designs involving dying, shaving, sculpting, braiding, and extensions.

White customers at the Toy Warehouse seemed frequently unnerved by their interactions with the clerks in the store. One time at the Toy Warehouse a white woman customer stopped my coworker Gail to ask for a gift suggestion for a ten-year-old boy. Gail, who was swiftly walking across the floor to deal with another customer's request, practically shouted at her, "Don't ask me about no boys; I got girls, not sons!" and then took off. The white woman looked startled at the response and maybe even a bit mortified. What she didn't know was that Gail found a coworker who had sons to answer the woman's question. The caring, efficiency, and sense of humor of my coworkers at the Toy Warehouse often went unnoticed by white customers.

Realizing that white customers in particular treated them with disrespect and even disdain, my African American coworkers developed interactional skills to minimize their involvement with them. I noticed at the service desk that the black women who worked there didn't smile or act concerned when customers came up for complaints or returns. They did their work well and efficiently (or at least as efficiently as possible given the myriad demands on their energies when they were at the service desk), but they did not exude a sense that they really cared. Rather, they looked suspicious, or bored, or resigned, or maybe a little miffed. That might be a defense mechanism. If they looked solicitous, then the customers would walk all over them. Over time I learned that this attitude of ennui or suspicion was cultivated as a way to garner respect for their work. It was saying, "This isn't my problem, it's your problem, but I will see what can be done to fix it." If workers were more gung-ho and it turned out that the problem couldn't be fixed, then they would look incompetent, which was the assumption that too many white customers were willing to make of black women. So they made it look as if the problem were insurmountable, and then when they did resolve it (which was most of the time) they garnered a little bit of respect. But it was at the cost of appearing unfriendly, so the store got hit with bad customer service evaluations.

With experience, I developed my own set of facial gestures and attitudes to manage customers. At the register, I learned to look cheerful unless there was a void and I had to wait for a manager to respond to a page, in which case I became expressionless and looked off to the distance, like a computer in shutdown mode. If you acted impatient, I learned, the customers would become impatient. At the service desk, I learned to act like a student. The customers were there to return or exchange something, and they had to explain why to get their refunds. To do this work effectively, I found that the best technique was to bow your head a little but raise your eyebrows and look into the eyes of the customer. No smiling and no frowning. This made you look a little skeptical but also subservient. I thought it also made you look stupid. You had to listen to the stories but not act as if you cared and/or were interested and then efficiently process the request. If the customers requested something that was against store policy, you just had to report that without sounding apologetic or giving the impression that the rule was wrong. That was just the rule, it was store policy, no exceptions. If they argued, you called a manager. This kind of affectless performance kept customers under control and lessened the likelihood that they would be insulting or make a scene.

Manipulating customers through self-presentation constitutes an informal "feeling rule" (Hochschild 1983). These techniques for displaying affect were developed by workers to manage and minimize difficult customer interactions. I call them informal rules because management would prefer that workers always convey serious concern and solicitude. This was the case at both stores. With few exceptions, workers at Diamond Toys accepted this directive, but many workers at the Toy Warehouse resisted it, recognizing that, if they were African Americans, adopting an attitude of servility would reinforce racism among shoppers. The informal rules were sensitive to race and gender dynamics in a way that management rules could not be. Different groups had to use different means to do their jobs.

Moreover, the stratification of the jobs at the store meant that we all had different levels of formal and informal power to resolve situations. White men had the most power in the stores. The store directors in both places where I worked were white men who could and did trump any decision made by managers or sales associates. Sales associates had virtually no options for resolving disputes. Measures intended to keep us from stealing also prevented us from dealing with customer complaints or special requests. We couldn't offer small discounts or make up a price when the tag was missing, for example, because doing so would make the store vulnerable to employee theft. Thus maintaining control was dependent on the race, gender, and organizational authority of both workers and customers.

INTERACTION BREAKDOWN: SOCIAL CONTROL IN THE TOY STORE

It may seem anathema to talk about power and control in the context of toy shopping. But customers frequently misbehaved in the stores where I worked. They didn't just throw fits at the service desk; every day I witnessed customers ripping open packages, hiding garbage, spilling Cokes, and generally making a mess of the store. One of my coworkers at Diamond Toys even found a dirty diaper on a shelf. There is a sort of gleeful abandon that some shoppers experience in a store. Barbara Ehrenreich (2001) describes how shoppers at Wal-Mart could tear down in minutes a clothing display that had taken her all day to arrange. She speculates that after full days of picking up after family members at home, some women shoppers like to experience a turn at being the messy ones.

As an older white woman, I could exercise some control over the extremes of this bad behavior. I could stand nearby, for example, and the customer might notice me and guiltily try to stuff the toy back into the box or replace the dozen toys she had pulled off the shelf. We weren't allowed to confront customers, even if we suspected them of stealing or destroying the merchandise, but we were expected to develop subtle ways to control them. I couldn't do this as well as my male coworkers could, but I was definitely more respected (and feared) than my women coworkers who were African American, Asian, and Latina.

One example of this involved Thelma, who was about fifty years old and was one of the two African American salesclerks at Diamond Toys. In the break room we talked about how rich the people were who shopped at the store. She said she easily got them to spend a lot of money, and she gave an example of how recently she had talked people into spending over $200. She said she was really good with the kids; she got them to behave by threatening to take away their toys. Their mothers were so grateful they sometimes asked her to come home with them and work for them. While she was proud of her selling ability, at the same time this particular reaction upset her. The women's offers clearly drew on cultural conventions linking black women to domestic service and to the "mammy" stereotype in particular. Thelma said that she objected to being treated like a servant. She said that the day before a customer had called her a "bitch" to one of the managers. She had asked the customer not to sit on the display tables because they were not sturdy and we had all been instructed to keep people off them. She asked her to not sit there in a polite way, but the woman got mad and complained to the manager, "That bitch told me to move. What if I had been disabled?" Thelma saw this treatment as racist and sexist. She said, "I am not her bitch," meaning her servant.

I witnessed similar mistreatment of my African American co-workers at the Toy Warehouse. One night, the store had officially closed, but I was still at my register. I saw Selma, an African American woman in her late forties, and told her, "There are still people in the store shopping." She said, "Oh no," and went to clear them out, saying, "We're closed, you must leave now, the registers are closing down!" As always, some refused to leave. These were usually white people. I was walking over to the service desk to close out my register when I saw that Doris, the night manager (an African American woman in her fifties), and Selma were escorting some people out. Later, when I was being audited in the manager's office, Selma came in very upset because the woman she and Doris had escorted out had spat out her chewing gum at her. Doris and Selma were appalled. Doris had said to them, "That is really disgusting, how could you do that?" And the woman said to Doris, "What is your name?" as if she were going to report her! This got Selma so angry she said, "If you take her name, take mine too," and showed her name tag. She told the woman that she would never be invited back to this store. Selma was very distressed. It was such a taboo to talk back to customers that she knew she could be fired for what she had said. Olive was there; she said that some people were going to be gross and disgusting and what could you do; clearly, Selma and Doris would not get in trouble over this. But I sensed it was doubly humiliating for Selma to have to be concerned that she would be punished for talking back to a white woman who had spat at her.

I didn't have too much trouble controlling white women. There was only one occasion when I felt threatened by one. Here are my field notes (from the Toy Warehouse):

> I had a really bad encounter with a customer. I was doing some restocking on the floor and turned a corner and saw a white woman with an open "Rollo" candy showing it to her husband (?) [and] saying, "This candy looks old [it had turned whitish with age], do you think it's safe to eat?" At that instant I walked up and caught her eye. I stayed where I was and straightened some shelf and they walked away, and the woman left the candy on a shelf. I picked up the candy and asked her, "Ma'am, did you pay for this?" And she got really belligerent and said, "Did you see me open it?" I knew right then that I shouldn't have said anything, so I walked away, with the idea of finding security. The woman shouted, "Are you going to put security on me?" and I didn't say anything. I ran into Allison back at my register and told her what hap-

pened. She said we shouldn't ever confront customers about stealing, but I explained how the encounter happened and she said, well, I didn't have a choice, it seemed, but just ignore it. At that time the woman, the man, and the ten-year-old girl who was with them were standing in the party section, close to my register. I said to Allison, "That's her," so Allison turned to look and she just smiled and said, "You can always tell. Just look at them; you know they came into this store to steal." The woman was overweight, with long fried permed hair that had a bad dye job, tight pedal pusher pants, and a large T-shirt. The little girl looked at me passively and expressionlessly, as if she was taking it all in. I didn't want to have an encounter with these people, so I said to Allison, "I am just going to the break room to wait a few minutes until they leave the store." I was in the break room only a couple of minutes when I heard a page from Jack (who was closing manager that night) for everyone on backup to go to their registers, so I went to mine. I saw the people talking to Jack, and when I walked by they pointed at me. I thought, "Oh, shit," but I just walked to my register and started checking people out. Jack never said anything to me, but later I ran into him and explained the situation, and he said, "Don't worry about it, but I will say a few things at closing about proper procedure." I asked, "What should I have done?" And he said, "We 'kill them with kindness.' " I should have said, "Ma'am, did you drop this?" and then "Can I help you find anything?" And then I should have notified security, who would have followed them through the store. I felt pretty bad about it.

I learned from this interaction never to confront a customer, even though I didn't suffer a reprimand (in fact, I felt more accepted afterwards, as if I had passed an initiation ritual). At the

Toy Warehouse, the work culture allowed for occasional trans-gression of the corporate code of customer service, especially in cases where misbehaving customers were not privileged by race, gender, or, in this instance, class.

The customers that I had the hardest time controlling were men. Men were outnumbered by women in both stores. At the Toy Warehouse, I saw them mostly on the weekend, which seemed to be the most popular time for fathers to come in with their children. (I often wondered if they were divorced fathers.) At Diamond Toys, I observed men tourists shopping with their families, businessmen buying small gifts for their children back home, and, during the Christmas season, men buying high-end toys for their wives. In general men seemed annoyed to be in the stores, and they sometimes acted annoyed with me, especially when they were unaccompanied by women. One white man at the Toy Warehouse tossed his shopping list at me when I was work-ing at the service desk. He expected me to assemble the items for him or get someone else to do it. One apparently very wealthy white man at Diamond Toys tossed his credit card at me while pointing to merchandise kept in the glass cases. I had to scurry after him to keep up with his numerous demands. Some men were just mean. On two occasions at Diamond Toys, men demanded to use my telephone, which the store had strict rules against. I said they weren't allowed to use it, and they just reached over the counter and did it anyway. I was terrified that Dorothy would walk by and yell at me, maybe even fire me. One time during the Christmas rush a white man complained to me about the wait at my register, an uncommon occurrence at Diamond Toys. I ex-plained that two of the workers hadn't shown up that day. He told me I should fire them. (Why he thought I had this power I couldn't guess.) On another occasion at Diamond Toys, a business professor in town for a professional convention was upset because a Barney sippy cup he wanted to buy was missing its price tag and I couldn't find it listed in the store inventory. He made me call over the store director and subjected both of us to a critique of store operations, which he threatened to write up and submit for publication to a business journal unless we sold him the sippy cup.

The sense of entitlement I experienced with these men customers was different from that which I encountered with white women customers. Perhaps the expectation that shopping was "women's work" made these men feel entitled to make me to do their shopping for them or reorganize the store to make it more convenient for them. To assert masculinity while engaging in this otherwise feminine activity seemed to require them to disrupt the routinized clerk-customer relationship.

In an extreme manifestation of this shopping masculinity, on three occasions (all at the Toy Warehouse), men threw merchandise in my direction, making me feel extremely threatened. Once a man threw a toy that resulted in my getting knocked in the head. Here is how I recorded the experience:

> The customer was a young African American, maybe thirty years old. When I first got to the service area he was trying to get a cash refund for a toy, baby Legos that came in a sand pail. Leticia, a twenty-three-year-old Latina who was working on the service desk, told him that he would have to accept a merchandise credit for the return because he didn't have a receipt. That made him very angry because he said he had just purchased the item a couple of days ago, so he demanded to talk to the manager. Leticia called the manager on duty, Jack, who was the heavily tattooed white man I met on my

first day of "training." Jack tried to explain the policy to the angry customer. I was watching this with half-attention because Leticia had asked me to answer the phone, which was ringing off the hook. The customer was yelling at Jack, using swear words, like "Fuck this shit, I don't give a damn!" Jack was trying to calm him down but also to say, "Please do not use that language, sir, this is a toy store." The customer was so angry he threw the toy on the counter, accidentally dislodging the phone, which came flying towards me, hitting me on the left side of my face and neck. I shrieked as I fell to the floor, and I thought I might cry (I didn't), and Jack said to Leticia, "Call the police NOW." The man started to walk toward the exit, but first he said, loudly, "If I don't get a cash refund, my kids won't eat tonight," and he left the store (without his merchandise!). Within minutes *three* police officers arrived and signaled me to come over to talk to them. They had found the man and wanted to know if I wanted to press charges. I decided not to. After all, men often threw things on that counter. It was this guy's bad luck that throwing something caused the phone to fly off the counter and hit me. Afterwards, when I was counting down my register for the night, Jack gave me a toy buck for "taking a hit" in the line of duty (thus entitling me to a free Coke).

This was not the only time that I witnessed Jack's inability to control African American men customers. I thought that overall Jack was a diligent and caring worker. I had noticed him on several occasions bonding with customers, including a very strange interaction with an African American man when they spent several minutes comparing their tattoos and ogling a Lara Croft action figure. ("She gives Barbie some competition!") Nevertheless, the particular race and gender dynamics that arose when Jack turned down the requests of African American men seemed to overwhelm the situations and cause them to spiral out of his control. I'm not sure, but I think some black men viewed Jack as a racist: they seemed to perceive that he didn't respect them, and they saw his power over them as illegitimate.[2]

But Jack was not the only one who threatened to call the police when black men customers became angry in the store. I noticed that this particular strategy for control was also used by the African American women supervisors and manager at the Toy Warehouse. Another night at the Toy Warehouse, it was after 9:00 P.M. and the store was supposed to be closed, but I was again stuck at my register to check out the last, straggling shoppers. Here are my field notes:

> An African American man, about forty, dressed kind of shabbily, entered the store at about 9:10. He came to my register in a hurry, slapped two Walkman CD players on the counter, and told me he needed to return them for cash. I told him, "Sir, the store is closed." He said to me, "Baby, I need the money tonight!" and I told him, even so, I could not process returns, only the service desk could, and there was no one there because the store was closed. He asked where the service desk was and I pointed to it, and he picked up his CD players and walked over there. I was frightened by his erratic and aggressive demeanor. I watched what happened as best I could. Leticia, who had returned to the service desk, called Kimberle, a twenty-nine-year-old African American supervisor, who heard the man's story and turned down his request, and the man argued with her. Kimberle took the CD players to the manager's office, to involve Olive. Somehow Kimberle convinced the man to leave the store, which was now locked. I thought the drama was over, but then I saw the man outside the store, knocking on the glass door, wanting to get in. Kimberle walked by my register as I was counting it down. I said,

"That man is still here," and she looked unfazed and said,
"Yes, I am still helping him." The man reentered the store
(which wasn't hard to do because the workmen on the night
shift were coming and going) and walked up to Kimberle.
She explained that they wouldn't be refunding his items.
Olive (who was watching the man on video surveillance)
came out of the office and said that if the man didn't leave
now they would be calling the police. He wanted his CD
players back, which were still in the manager's office. They
told him that if he left then Kimberle would retrieve the CD
players and take them outside to him. This was taking place
near my register (which was one of the ones closest to the
exit). Leticia came up and told me to take my till away, and
she handed me another one that was close by and told me to
take that one to the service desk too. Later she said she did
this to protect the tills from this man.

Afterwards, Olive told me that the guy was drunk, that
he reeked. She also said he was damn lucky to get the CD
players back because she was certain that he stole them.
There was some concern that the man was lurking outside,
so Kimberle watched each of us workers walk out of the
store after clocking out. But I noticed that I was the only
one who seemed unnerved; the others (like Leticia)
seemed kind of amused by it all or treated it as "all in a
day's work."

This episode illustrates how assumptions and stereotypes
guided the trading between store employees and customers. Some
customers were considered more demanding and harder to control than others, in particular, black men and white women. But
no one ever threatened to call the police on an angry white
woman. In general, only white women could count on being appeased; for them, acting out seemed to get the results they desired.

The fact that police were called to control only black men customers reveals underlying cultural assumptions about gender and race. Toy stores catered to white mothers, who were believed to be behaving virtuously—if not civilly—on behalf of their children. Black men, in contrast, were assumed to be violent by nature; their anger was seen as evidence of an underlying animal nature that had to be controlled.[3]

Thus white women's demands were satisfied because, from a corporate perspective, their anger was assumed to serve a legitimate end. They also were appeased because it was assumed that they had economic resources ($20,000 for each child!), an assumption that was almost never invoked in the case of black men. White women were immediately seen as potential spenders; black men, as potential thieves. In the overall retail environment, these racialized assumptions might extend to white and black people in general (Chin 2001), but in a toy store that catered to women in particular, we might predict this polarized race/gender dynamic to emerge.[4] Thus a shouting white woman got whatever she wanted and a shouting black man got threatened with arrest. (Other groups of customers, in my experience, didn't shout, with the notable exception of children.)

Some have argued that stealing and scamming in stores can be understood as a form of resistance to racism toward black consumers. This has certainly been the case in the past, when organized looting by African Americans expressed their collective anger at being excluded, mistreated, and/or overcharged by white merchants (Cohen 2003). Some of the customers caught stealing may have been motivated by such social and economic protest, but I don't have any way to know this. What I do know is that

African Americans were typically assumed to be scamming whenever they complained, returned merchandise, or made special requests. Whites were given the benefit of the doubt.

African American shoppers sometimes resisted what they perceived as discriminatory treatment in the stores. In one case, I was
accused of racism for sending a black customer to another register. I was in the electronics department of the Toy Warehouse
when an African American man approached me and asked if he
needed to check out there. I told him no, he could go to the main
registers. (Anyone could check out in the electronics department,
but those purchasing electronics had to use that register.) My next
customer, who was not black, then approached the counter, and I
proceeded to check him out. An African American woman observing this confronted me and asked why I had sent the other
man away. She thought I had refused to serve him because he was
black. I tried to explain, but I could tell that she wasn't convinced.

CONCLUSION

As a nation of consumers, we spend a great deal of time in stores
interacting with sales workers. In this chapter I have tried to
make a case for paying attention to these interactions as sites for
the reproduction of social inequality. I argue that where we shop
and how we shop are shaped by and bolster race, class, and gender inequalities.

Corporations script the customer-server interaction in ways
that are designed to appeal to a particular kind of customer. The
fun, child-centered Toy Warehouse aimed to attract middle-class
mothers who were looking for a wide assortment of toys at discount prices, while the sophisticated Diamond Toys catered to a

more discriminating, upper-class clientele. These corporate-driven agendas influenced who entered the stores as customers and also shaped the labor practices of the two stores. The Toy Warehouse attracted a dazzling mix of customers who were served by a mostly African American staff. At that store, my job was to swiftly and cheerfully process customer requests and check them out at the register. At Diamond Toys, in contrast, the service encounter was considered a more central part of my job. I was expected to provide "professional" advice to the well-to-do, mostly white clientele. It was not a coincidence that the majority of salesclerks at that store were white. Stores like Diamond Toys that marketed their "expert" staff might prefer to hire whites instead of African Americans because of the (presumed) racism of wealthy shoppers and a culture that associates professionalism with whiteness.

At my training sessions at the two stores, I learned scripts to follow in dealing with customers, ranging from lessons on how to process returns to the "five I's" of customer service. But actual interactions on the shopping floor strayed from these ideal rituals. Both clerks and customers drew on elaborate stereotypes in crafting their shopping practices, reflecting the existence of a "matrix of domination" that sorted individuals on the basis of race, gender, and class. Because of the matrix, white customers basically got whatever they wanted, and many developed a sense of shopping entitlement. Similarly, white workers were treated with more deference and respect, particularly by white shoppers.

When interactions broke down, the ability to repair them depended on the characteristics of the customer and worker. As a white woman, I had a different repertoire of control strategies than my African American women coworkers. They had to reckon with racist as well as sexist assumptions from irate white customers, while most of my difficulties were due to customer sexism. White men had more power in the stores, but they seemed to have difficulty managing and controlling black customers. Control was an achievement that had to be negotiated anew with each service interaction.

I realize that most of my examples of conflict are from the Toy Warehouse. I believe that conflict was more common there than at Diamond Toys. The unusually diverse mix of people in the Toy Warehouse often provoked misunderstandings, as when Gail shouted at the customer that she didn't have sons. Diamond Toys protected itself from conflict by catering to an upper-class clientele, thereby functioning much like a gated community. This is not to say that diversity always results in conflict, but it did at the Toy Warehouse because race, class, and gender differences were overlain by power differences within the store. Interactions between clerks and customers took place within a context where these differences had been used to shape marketing agendas, hiring practices, and labor policies—all of which benefited some groups (especially middle-class white women and men) over others.

From a sociological perspective, there is nothing inevitable about these categories or their meanings. Race, class, and gender are not inherent properties of individuals; they are socially constructed categories that derive their significance through human interactions. On rare instances, I experienced interactions with customers that transcended their ritualized forms and momentarily broke through the matrix of domination. I'll never forget one time a customer at the Toy Warehouse invited me to join her church. Normally I would be annoyed by such an offer, but in this context it made me so grateful I almost took her up on it. I recorded the episode in my field notes:

> An African American woman was in the store with her husband and two kids. I gave the kids balloons and chatted with them a little bit. Then the woman asked me if I worked on Sunday. I said yes, and she said, too bad, she liked to invite friendly people to their church. I was so amazed by this glimmer of mutual recognition that I eagerly replied, "I don't work every Sunday! What is your church?" She gave me her business card with her home phone number written on it and the name of the church with its meeting times.

Exceptional experiences like this give me hope that the retail environment can be structured differently, to encourage mutual respect in clerk-customer interactions instead of a fight for domination and control.

Currently, however, manipulation and exploitation are the modus operandi of the retail industry. Corporations structure the clerk-customer interaction along these lines. The advertising strategy of the Toy Warehouse encouraged customers to expect friendly and efficient service, but the pay and working conditions provided by the store provoked staff resentment or indifference instead. Workers then bore the brunt of customer anger when their expectations were not met. Workers' frustrations—already high because of their powerlessness—were only exacerbated when the complaining customer was a member of a privileged group and the worker was not. At Diamond Toys, overt conflict may have been absent, but manipulation and exploitation were commonplace. Customers entered the store willing to pay more for what they thought was expert advice about high-quality merchandise. But the corporation encouraged high turnover among the staff and provided virtually no training about the merchandise they sold (most of which was available at discount stores). Let the buyer beware: corporations lie to enhance their profits.

Is there another way to organize the clerk-customer relationship?[5] One could imagine a different organization of toy stores that was not driven by niche marketing. Buyers and sellers could be imagined as part of a team, each dependent on the other for the satisfaction of their needs. Corporations could provide customers with trustworthy information about the merchandise they sell. This would require investing in workers and rewarding them for their knowledge and service skills. Customers would have to recognize the effort and dignity of all workers and accept that they were not always right. They would have to recognize that low prices often mean high levels of exploitation, not only of those who make the merchandise they buy, but also of those who take their money at the checkout counter.

These changes describe a major cultural shift but not one without precedent. Stores currently exist that promote mutual recognition between diverse groups of service workers and customers. I can think of several in my own shopping experience that fit this description, although most tend to be small and some are employee owned. In these establishments, the conditions are provided for relationships of trust and respect to develop between clerks and their customers. The fact that they can exist and thrive suggests that retail itself is not the problem. It is the current social organization of retailing that promotes domination and control. Imagining an alternative is the first, necessary step to making it better.

5

KIDS IN TOYLAND

Everyone knows that children cost a lot of money. They also spend a lot of money. Those under thirteen spent over $40 billion of their own money in 2002, compared to just over $17 billion in 1994 (Center for a New American Dream 2003; McNeal 1999). They influence adult purchases as well. James McNeal, a children's marketing expert, estimates that kids twelve and under influence around $500 billion worth of adults' spending. Perhaps it is not surprising, then, that shopping is the number one leisure-time activity for most American children (Kline 1993, 176).

Experts are divided over the question of whether all of this shopping and spending is good for children (Zelizer 2002). They grapple over whether children should be protected from the marketplace and hence from capitalist exploitation in order to preserve their "innocence" or socialized into market relationships to make them savvy customers empowered to make their own choices and influence the kinds of commodities available for their consumption. Postmodernist theorists favor the latter type of inquiry; not surprisingly, so do marketing researchers. As Dan Cook (2000, 503) observes: "The view of the child as a willful, knowledgeable, and desiring agent who is making her/his own decisions and exercising self-expression through the medium of the commodity form is, of course, favored by those who work in and profit from children's industries."

Zelizer and Cook are leading the way to a new type of inquiry that transcends this either-or debate. They are interested in exploring how children actually relate to the marketplace through ethnographic studies. Here the question isn't whether children should be engaged in market activity. Rather, it is how social relationships shape children's economic activities and how children respond to efforts to control them.

In this chapter, I focus on adults' efforts to shape children's toy-shopping experience. Children must be taught how to shop; this isn't a behavior that comes naturally. I argue that the lessons learned in the toy store have repercussions throughout society. How we shop is shaped by and contributes to social inequality. Obviously this happens in the economic sense: rich people can buy more things than poor people can. They also have more choices of where to shop. In recent years, inner-city neighborhoods have experienced a decline in retail tenants, constricting the shopping options of many poor people. As retail centers have shifted to suburban locations, they have become inaccessible (often by design) to those who lack private means of transportation (Cohen 2003).

My goal in this chapter, however, is to discuss, not the economic inequalities that are reflected and reproduced in shopping, but rather the cultural norms and practices that legitimize inequality. To make this argument, I draw on Pierre Bourdieu's theory of culture.[1] Bourdieu sought to understand how stratified social systems persist and reproduce themselves without powerful resistance and often without the conscious recognition of their members. He argues that *culture* is the key to understanding inequality: cultural resources, processes, and institutions hold individuals and groups in competitive hierarchies of domination. All cultural forms—including styles of dress, eating habits, religion, science, philosophy, and even toys—embody interests and function to enhance social distinctions, and thus social inequality (Swartz 1997).

Culture does this by transforming practices based on economic interest into practices that seem to be disinterested. That is, rich people are able to use their resources in ways that legitimate their power. They convert their economic capital into cultural capital—educational degrees, appreciation for high art and music, sophisticated sensibilities and taste in fashion, food, and decoration. This conversion process is facilitated by experts or specialists, including intellectuals. By the conversion of economic capital (money) into cultural capital (proper values, refined sensibilities, good taste), an illegitimate power is transformed into a legitimate power. Dominated people tend to accede status and control to those who possess cultural capital because they seem deserving of the respect, deference, and services of others. In other words, elites who possess large amounts of cultural capital are believed to deserve their power by virtue of their personal qualities—their superior intellect, refinement, personalities, and so on. Thus class divisions are converted into status divisions: status is "a sort of veneer that legitimates class inequality by presenting it under the guise of disinterestedness" (Swartz 1997, 45).

Most people—both elites and nonelites—are not aware of this process of cultural legitimation, a process Bourdieu and Wacquant (1992) call "symbolic violence." Power goes "misrecognized" in society, a concept akin to Marx's notion of false consciousness. We can thus reproduce inequality and domination—even our own domination by others—without knowing it.

These processes play out in our consumer practices. As Ellen Seiter (1993) has shown, shopping involves making creative choices and distinguishing between nice and bad, beautiful and tacky, refined and banal. Through the careful selection of clothes, food, and toys, consumers express their allegiance to particular values and norms, thereby converting economic power into status distinctions. Making the "wrong" choices can make a person seem undeserving of social respect or even immoral.

In toy shopping, this kind of status distinction is reflected in the decisions of both where to shop and what to buy. Diamond Toys, with its reputation for selling refined toys to sophisticated and discriminating adult consumers, conveyed high status to shoppers. Buying at Diamond Toys offered proof of one's cultural refinement. (Many shoppers requested extra shopping bags displaying the company logo.) Shopping at the Toy Warehouse, in contrast, conveyed no such superior status. Bourdieu would argue that this status distinction both obscures and legitimizes economic inequality. It obscures inequality by making it seem that shoppers at Diamond Toys simply have better "taste" than shoppers at the Toy Warehouse, when really they have more privilege (due to class and race inequality). It furthermore legitimizes the belief that those with highly cultivated tastes ought to be rewarded with superior service and merchandise. In this way, wealth disparity in our society is transformed into a matter of "choice" and "taste," not domination and inequality.

Just as some groups seem to know the "right" places to shop, other groups always seem to make the "wrong" shopping choices.

Ann Norton (1993, 56) argues that women, African Americans, and immigrants are often criticized for their shopping practices. They are seen as especially "prone to extravagance . . . , full of desires, easily lured by the pretty and the prestigious, seduced by advertising, and given to consumption and display." Their choices are taken as evidence of their low social and moral worth, which then justifies their economic marginality.

Norton (1993) doesn't include children in her analysis, but they certainly fit. Children are among those groups "on the periphery [who] are commonly excluded, by law, custom, or the lack of resources, from full participation in American economic structures" (56). Consequently, their consumer choices typically are considered unrefined and mark them as undeserving and in need of control.

Elizabeth Chin (2001) takes up this point in her study of black urban youth. This group is often criticized for "spending money they haven't earned on things they shouldn't have" (43), such as high-priced sneakers and flashy jewelry. Minority youth in particular are seen as destructive, greedy, and out-of-control consumers, highly susceptible to commodity fetishism, willing to compromise their health and well-being to acquire expensive yet tacky commodities. Ironically, the "outrageous" and unrefined consumer practices of marginal groups can become mainstream and "acceptable" once corporations appropriate them, repackage them, and sell them to the middle-class consumer. But before this happens, the consumer practices of minority groups are taken as emblematic of their inferior moral qualities.

In contrast, the extravagant tastes of the rich are not typically seen as reflecting character or group flaws. This is because their "choices" set the standards of high culture and define what does and what does not constitute cultural sophistication. These are the standards and values emulated by the middle class, who tend to look down on the "street" values attributed to minority youth and up to the "refined" lifestyles of the rich and famous. Chin (2001, 12) writes that many middle-class people assume that "if only those [poor] people would . . . want the right things, dress appropriately, buy the right foods, they too could be middle class." Their economic condition is thus explained as a consequence of their unrefined consumer choices.

Here is an example of how this works. Once when I was working in the electronics department of the Toy Warehouse, a poor African American family came in to buy a trendy, violent video game cartridge that cost $50, which they purchased with a gift card. This indicated either that someone had given them a gift certificate to buy anything they wanted in the store or that they had returned merchandise for store credit. (When poor people used gift cards, the clerks would assume that they had stolen some items in the store and later had tried to return them for a cash refund. Because they didn't have a receipt, they received store credit in the form of a gift card instead.) There were four children with their parents; all of them were dirty, and the youngest, around four, didn't have pants or shoes. My reaction at the time was to criticize the parents. What terrible parents, I thought, buying a tacky video game instead of clothes for their children!

What's wrong with this interpretation?

First, the definition of the video game as "tacky" is a reflection of who is buying it, not some inherent quality of the object. Objects in material culture do not have the same meaning for everyone in every context. If the same video game were available at Diamond Toys and upper-class people bought it, then it would not be a degraded object. Second, this interpretation assumes that this family's consumer choice was wasteful and ignorant. But I don't know why this family bought this video. It could have been for a number of reasons. This could have been a special treat saved up for by the family. It could have been an investment that the family would then charge others to play. It could have been a reward for some achievement they were celebrating. If the gift card was indeed the result of a prior theft, it could have been a form of resistance to capitalism. Or it could have been an irresponsible waste of scarce resources. To assume only the latter is to bolster social and economic inequality.

Ann Norton (1993) argues that in a consumer society like ours consumption is one of the principal means available to participate in public discourse and hence to achieve a political voice. The fact that certain groups are deemed unworthy of participating in this discourse makes the act of shopping an act of resistance for them. She writes, "Consumption thus becomes, for these groups, not merely a way but the principal, often the only, way in which they could represent themselves in the world or interject themselves in public discourse" (57).

But even if their purchase represented some sort of resistant meaning that challenged the social order, buying an expensive toy ultimately bolsters social inequality. Norton notes the irony that the attempts by peripheral groups to acquire power and self-determination through the acquisition of consumer goods merely increase their indebtedness to those who are economically powerful. Consumerism sustains the capitalist enterprise that produces economic inequality in the first place. Thus, even though the conspicuous consumption of the poor and marginal can be symbolically subversive, the current organization of consumerism supports the very system of inequality that results in the impoverishment of many and the enrichment of the few.

The role of the social scientist, according to Bourdieu, is to reveal the unequal power relations that are sustained by cultural legitimation practices such as these. In the context of shopping, this means questioning why certain consumers are considered "smarter" than others and certain choices are considered "better" than others. If Bourdieu is right, publicly exposing how certain groups have more power than others in determining quality and value will undermine the cultural forms of legitimation. But, he warns us, social actors are likely to resist this interpretation, insisting instead that their choices reflect some true and universal good. Bourdieu maintains that there is no such thing as a superior, pure, or innocent vantage point in a system based on domination. Everyone participates in the struggle for distinction and status: in every arena of life, we all take part in defining what is a valued characteristic, and we all attempt to achieve distinction. In other words, we all participate in defining what is and is not valuable and worth struggling for, and then we compete for these things. In this sense, we are all caught in the web of domination and subordination.

This struggle to define what is valuable is played out every day in the toy store. Adults and children are often locked in battle over the norms and values of shopping—evident in the number of temper tantrums I witnessed at the checkout line. Adults try to teach children a set of ideal norms regarding consumerism, while children struggle to satisfy their own sense of what is good and valuable. Toys are an obvious battleground, since they constitute a "lingua franca" of childhood (Seiter 1993), the means through which children forge their peer group alliances and stake out their independence from their parents. Children learn, resist, appeal, and negotiate the lessons of toy shopping, often to their parents' dismay. In very public disputes, they highlight the norms, making them more accessible to the sociologist's eye.

Adults also experience conflicts over shopping and consumerism, but they are more likely to be played out in private, or else internally. A burgeoning psychological literature suggests that shopping meets unmet emotional needs for many adults, especially women (Hine 2002). Because in a consumer society we acquire things to express who we are and who we want to be, the experience of shopping can bring out deep ambivalence about our self-worth and our relationships. This can make shopping a compulsion for some and a traumatic experience for others. Yet somehow we are more disturbed when these characteristics are expressed openly in children. As Stephen Kline (1993) observes, when children feel the need to wear a designer label, or when they fight over a coveted object, adults feel that something is awry. Kline writes, "[I]t is easiest to recognize the deeper paradoxes of our consumer culture when it is refracted back to us through the mirror of childhood" (12). Adults' attempts to control children in the toy store and to teach them how to be good consumers can, in this sense, serve as a window into the cultural norms and psychological ambivalence that affect us all.

SHOPPING 101

Teaching children how to shop at the most basic level involves lessons in accounting and money management. The kids I observed in the Toy Warehouse often had their own money and were expected to pay for their own toys. This was the case even with very young children. Here is an excerpt from my field notes:

> A pregnant African American woman in her thirties came to my register with her two children. They were clearly middle to upper middle class. The children checked out first: the boy, probably seven, bought his toys (trucks and machines) and paid with a $20 bill. Kids are funny when they pay, they aren't sure how to do it (the younger ones at least). They give the money right away; I have to tell them to wait until I tell them how much they owe. Mom was standing watch and making sure it went right. He got about $7 back, and I counted out his change to make it seem like a math lesson. Next the eight-year-old daughter bought her toys and also paid with a $20 bill. I made a comment to Mom about them spending their special birthday money or special gift, and she told me, no, they always paid with their own money. The daughter knew how to do a transaction. She bought a baby doll stroller and other baby doll toys that came out to about $19.50, so she had only a little bit of change compared to her brother, and she clearly felt accomplished about doing that. Next it was the mom's turn to buy her things, and she bought (real) baby things, like bibs and formula. A white woman behind her in line informed her that there was a $1 off coupon for two bibs in the sales circular, and they rushed to find it. I said, "Take your time, don't worry," and we eventually found it and rang up the sale. The women clearly bonded over this moment.

The overt lesson in shopping in this example involved learning how to conduct a transaction and audit the cashier. This part of shopping is highly routinized, and many adults consider it important that children learn how to do it at an early age. Kline (1993) points out that whereas an earlier generation of parents emphasized the importance of saving, today's parents expect their children to learn how to spend money in order to learn responsibility and consumer skills.[2] According to marketing researchers, children are shopping alone at very young ages: one study finds most children have shopped alone by age five, and by the age of eight, the average U.S. child is in a shop alone three times per week (Kline 1993, 182). This helps to explain why learning to audit the cashier is a top priority for many parents.

But the more covert instruction or hidden curriculum in this example includes lessons about gender and consumerism. The "hidden curriculum" is a concept borrowed from the education literature that refers to the implicit lessons learned in schools. The point of the concept is to reveal how social inequalities—in particular, race, class, and gender inequalities—are reproduced in informal and unnoticed ways. In this example, the hidden curriculum teaches that shopping is mothers' work, part of a system of care work that women do for their families. This lesson is reflected in the items selected for purchase: Mom and daughter bought "baby items" to care for other family members, real or imagined, while the son purchased vehicles evocative of masculine independence. Shopping is also an opportunity to bond with other women; in this case, with me, the cashier, and with the other woman in line who shared the information about the coupon. For many women, part of the enjoyment of shopping is the chance to connect with other women, including strangers involved in similar care work for their families.

Also in this example are lessons about consumerism. Children are taught to maximize acquisitions, or get the most stuff for the money. In this case, the lesson is reinforced by the mother's use of coupons. It is also reflected in the girl's achievement of spending close to, but not more than, the money she had, marking her as a more skillful shopper than her younger brother (a skill that is celebrated on the popular, long-running game show *The Price Is Right*). But interestingly, this value contradicts a second overt lesson, about the importance of "good value." Young children do not notice if something costs $10 or $100, and they don't distinguish well-made goods from ones that are likely to fall apart as soon as they are out of the box. Parents try to influence children's choices by steering them to what they think is a better value, in terms of both price and quality. This is a more difficult lesson to teach and to learn.

For example, one time at the Toy Warehouse, I observed a child about five or six buying a junky toy that cost around $19. His mother explained that this meant he would have to spend all the allowance he had saved up. She asked him if he was sure that this was what he wanted to do, and he said "Yeah!" so he went ahead and bought it.

The child had no idea what money was, but he fully understood the toy. This struck me as an especially vivid example of the fetishism of commodities. Very young children were learning the magical properties of money: bits of paper could be converted into spectacular objects. Toys for young children are marketed with this sensibility in mind. Merchandisers put a lot of effort into analyzing toy placement and packaging to appeal to children's sensibilities, and it is very effective. Kids are complete suckers for fancy packaging, especially for cheap toys covered in hard clear plastic with images of laughing children on the box.

But children are not the only ones who fetishize commodities. At Diamond Toys, adults seemed more likely than children to confer special power or charisma on the items offered for sale. This was especially true of the European toys, such as the Brio train set, a very expensive wooden train (all parts sold separately). They were willing to pay more because it was Brio. A wide variety of objects at Diamond Toys were coveted by adults for their special, magical properties, even though the same items were available at the Toy Warehouse. One time a frantic woman came up to me and asked if we still sold a clock that she had purchased there two years ago. The one she had needed replacement. She explained that the clock counted down the minutes ("5—4—3 . . . to go"), which was perfect for bath time because her child would mind the clock and not her. I couldn't parse out who was fetishizing the commodity in this instance; clearly, both parents and children do this. But it did seem evident that the marketing strategy of Diamond Toys—with its emphasis on status and exclusivity—appealed more to adults' fantasies, while the Toy Warehouse appealed more to the fantasies of children.

At the Toy Warehouse, middle-class parents were often appalled by the kitschy toys that their children coveted and tried to interest them in other things. Children retained their authority as the ultimate decision makers in these instances. Most children seemed willing to accept more toys but never to relinquish their first choice. I say "most" instead of all because on rare occasions I witnessed children who were completely uninterested in toys despite the urging of their parents. However, this was something I only observed at Diamond Toys. Here is an example:

> A family came in [to Diamond Toys] to buy a push-type fire truck. These are little vehicles made out of molded plastic that young kids (around two to three) can sit on and push with their feet and steer with little steering wheels. Mom and

Dad were there with two little kids in tow, one about three, getting the fire truck, and a baby in arms, younger than one. The mom couldn't decide which truck to buy, the red one or the blue one. She asked the kid, "Which one do you want?" The kid seemed completely bored and listless. They put him on one of the display models, where he sat, not smiling, not playing, apparently unimpressed. The mom kept trying to get him to decide, showing him the features of each one (bells, dials, horns, etc.). Eventually she decided that since he was sitting on the blue one he should get that. So we found it in the box and I went to ring her up. She kept trying to get the kid interested in the thing: "Here's your new truck!" "This is for you!" But the kid stayed expressionless. The mom told me that the kid was totally spoiled and that it was his grandparents' fault. He got whatever he wanted, she said, so I jokingly asked, did she want to buy more, then? (Here I was doing the "include" stage of the Five I's.) She also bought him a little backpack that was in the shape of a stuffed animal. The purchase came to over $60. The parents sighed and walked out with their silent kids.

Purchases at Diamond Toys often had this "top-down" quality: adults would select the toy (or toys), and the child then would be encouraged to appreciate its superior properties. In the vast majority of instances they were successful; children would gratefully or greedily accept the gift. In the Bourdieuian frame, these adults could be seen as trying to cultivate sophisticated tastes in their children, providing them with all-important cultural capital they need to succeed in a class-stratified society. However, it is unlikely that this is how adults see their own behavior. Many parents buy toys simply to express their love. In this particular instance with the fire trucks, the child's indifferent response to his parents' gift suggests the tragic possibility that they are unable to communicate their affection to their child.

In contrast, the following transaction, which also took place at Diamond Toys, came closer to achieving this ideal. (I recall including this in my field notes because it seemed so exceptional.)

A Mexican mother and her ten-year-old daughter came to my register to buy a little battery-operated lollipop with some cartoon character on it. It wasn't expensive; the total was about $5. The mother didn't speak English, but the daughter did a little bit. They were very polite at the counter, as if I were helping them instead of them helping me (the usual attitude). The mom smiled brilliantly at me when I returned her change. I watched them leave and the daughter gave her mom a very warm hug and kiss to thank her for this special treat, and the mom just was beaming. It was a really special moment, like the "pure" relationship that advertisers usually promise through consumption.

Every consumer purchase holds out the promise of intimacy. Adults often buy toys for children to express their affection and appreciation, which they hope will be reciprocated. Many children do not fully understand this, much to their parents' painful frustration. It is a lesson that has to be learned.

BARGAINING FOR TOYS

While for the most part younger children were profligate, I observed that older middle-class children were often reluctant to spend their own money even when they had it. I was often amazed at the older children's negotiating skills with their parents. They bargained over what to buy and whose money was going to pay for it. Here is one example:

A white woman in her forties was shopping with her twelve-year-old daughter. They were looking for "My Generation Barbie," and they came to my register saying they couldn't find it; maybe we were sold out? I told them I thought we had it and left my register to help them look for it. We couldn't find it on the Barbie wall, but we did find "Jewel Barbie" and the girl said that her friend (this was a present for a friend) had specified that she wanted either Jewel Barbie or My Generation Barbie, so they would just purchase this one. But Mom insisted that we find My Generation, and I offered to find someone who could tell us about it. I looked for my coworker who was in charge of the section (eighteen-year-old Karelin), but, not surprisingly, she was nowhere to be found, and I came back and said no luck. The little girl was insisting that Jewel Barbie was just fine, but the mom wasn't so sure. So I said I would go to the front and we could search the inventory. The mom said great, and they followed me, but then, lo and behold, we ran right into the display of My Generation Girl (not Barbie after all), and they were very happy about this, especially the mom. (It is a really cool doll, with lots of tiny plastic accessories, like a skateboard and Walkman for the doll.) I went back to the register, and a couple of minutes later they were there purchasing the doll (plus some candy that the daughter had picked up—the mom tried to talk her out of that but it was too late—"You don't need candy"— "Yes I do," and besides, this was a cool, special kind of candy, a hollow chocolate ball the size of a racquetball filled with M&Ms). It was interesting to me how they paid: the girl got out a wad of cash and pulled out a ten, and the mom paid the rest (it cost about $25 total). So the deal was that the girl had to pay $10 of her "own" money for the doll for her friend (she didn't have to pay for the candy, though).

This arrangement was very curious to me, but over time I noticed that several middle-class children engaged in elaborate accounting methods with their parents. Some parents matched children's contributions toward a purchase dollar for dollar. These techniques enabled parents to exert control over their children's consumer choices while at the same time increasing the children's purchasing power.

In this case it was striking that the child appeared to be a more mature shopper than the mother. She was ready to settle on the first appropriate gift they found, while the mother seemed a little bit crazed to me. But the mother was teaching another lesson about consumerism to her daughter: the most important aspect of shopping was the comparison. We express ourselves and our personal feelings about the people we care about through the gifts we give them. The gift isn't meaningful if we don't choose it because then it wouldn't be a reflection of the individual giver. Of course, in this case, it was just the illusion of "choice," since the recipient of the gift was very specific about what she wanted. So the only way to "personalize" a gift was to compare it with the other items on the wish list. A quasi-choice was better than no choice at all.

A third lesson in the hidden curriculum of shopping is evident in this interaction. The mother was teaching the daughter about the server-customer relationship. This is something I experienced only with white women, and very occasionally white men:

they would treat me like their personal servant. Retail work is a form of "service," but I had never made the connection to the historical meaning of this term until I worked at this job. Some shoppers at both stores would treat me like their personal valet. I was supposed to stop whatever I was doing (including helping other customers) to wait on them, and I would never be dismissed: they would expect me to stand by and wait for them to decide and then help them with the purchase. As I noted in the previous chapter, this style of interacting with customers was central to the marketing agenda of Diamond Toys, in contrast to the discounter strategy of the Toy Warehouse. But white customers at both stores would often expect a high level of solicitous attention. When I started working retail I would find myself asking the customers, "Will that be all?" (in other words, "Can I go now?"), but later I learned to say, "If there is anything else you need, I'll be up at the desk," because, if given the choice, these shoppers would never let me go. The young girl in this transaction was learning this way of treating service workers. I think she was a little mortified by her mother's behavior, but in the end her mother's effort paid off because they found the special doll. She learned a lesson about the importance of controlling service workers and demanding their attention.

At the Toy Warehouse, where this incident took place, children paid at the register perhaps a third of the time. This was an extremely rare occurrence at Diamond Toys. Although there were always plenty of children in the store, I never witnessed one paying for his or her own toy. Parents seemed to be reserving the expensive toy store for themselves, tightly controlling any purchases for children.

It was not uncommon at the Toy Warehouse to witness children engaging in elaborate negotiations with their parents, something I rarely witnessed at Diamond Toys. Here is one example:

An African American father in his mid-thirties was shopping with his ten-year-old daughter and six-year-old son. He was buying toys for each of them. The boy was getting a couple of trucks, and the girl got a single Barbie (the $6 kind) plus a Mary-Kate and Ashley set of dolls with a playscape included. I rang up his purchases and it came to about $60, and he said, "Whoa, what happened there?" I looked at the tape and told him that the expensive part of the purchase was the Mary-Kate and Ashley doll set, which cost about $35. He looked at his daughter and said, "What's this? Bait and switch? That isn't what you had picked earlier. This is too much." She said that she really wanted this instead. The dad said no, she could have the other thing that he had already approved, but that other thing was long gone. She ran back out into the store and brought back another doll, this one a black Barbie in a laundry setting (Barbies were sold in every room of the house). Clever, because this was holding up the line and that put the parents on the spot having to make the decisions in front of a crowd. He asked how much it was, and it was $25, so he was unsure, but he said, "Well, OK, if you take out the other $6 Barbie you can have this one." So that is what happened. The girl managed to negotiate from what was originally a $15 total purchase up to a $25 purchase. She did this by sneaking in a $35 purchase, which she knew she had a very slim chance of getting, but because of that initial sticker shock, her dad was prepared for the toy that was somewhat less expensive (but more than he wanted to pay). I thought about how skilled a negotiator this girl was going to be. In retrospect, I recalled that she had tried to distract me

and her dad during the transaction so that we wouldn't notice the expensive Mary-Kate and Ashley; as soon as I
checked the tape she acted as if she had been busted and was
disappointed in that.

Children in the Toy Warehouse would often try to increase the
number of purchases or to upgrade the value of their purchase.
One way they did this was to sneak an item onto the register
counter at checkout. The Toy Warehouse catered to this practice
by placing toys and trinkets right next to the counter at the child's
eye level.

Although many children complained that their parents didn't
buy them enough, I was constantly amazed at the amount of
money parents were willing to spend on toys—although some experienced sticker shock, as in this example:

An Asian American mom was buying Game Boy video games
for her four-year-old son and eight-year-old son, who was
with a friend. The younger child picked one that cost $50
and two others that cost $20 each. The mother said, "You
can't have all of them." The kid wasn't going to budge, he
wanted them all. Mom insisted, "You can either have the expensive one or the other two," and the kid chose the expensive one. At that time the older boys came up to the counter
and made fun of the kid for choosing one instead of two, but
the little kid put his foot down and that was what he got. The
mother said to me, "These games are really expensive," and I
agreed. She said the problem was that the kids wouldn't share
the games so she had to buy multiple copies of the same
game. In fact, she told me, the older son already owned a
copy of the game the younger son was purchasing and the
two older children had bought copies of the same game. She
was clearly disappointed in them for not sharing.

In the toy stores, sharing was never an option. Although adults bought toys to solidify bonds with children, each toy was intended for a specific individual. The value and worth of the toy were elided with the value and worth of the person receiving the toy. Several adults who were buying toys for more than one child were obsessed with ensuring that the value of the toys they bought would be identical, presumably so they couldn't be accused of playing favorites. The easiest way of ensuring this was to buy two (or more) of the same thing. I often encountered this attitude at Diamond Toys. Adults buying gifts for siblings would insist on equivalents.

Today, two separate customers asked me for help to find presents for siblings. In both cases these were white men who said that the kids had to be given identical presents or else they would fight. One man was looking for Harry Potter figurines for his two sons, and we didn't have two of the same so he wouldn't buy them. Another was looking for gifts for two girls, daughters of a close friend he was visiting in the city. They were aged three and seven and he wanted to buy the same for both. At first he selected two identical Madeline felt doll kits (like paper dolls but made out of felt). He asked me if this toy would be appropriate for both girls, and I was unsure. We walked around the store thinking about alternatives. In the end he settled on a picnic basket for the older one and the felt kit for the younger one. He was really stressed out about it. I told him he shouldn't be stressed out in a toy store, but he was worried that he would cause trouble in the family he was visiting. He was lugging his suitcase around the store with him. He was exhausted, having flown in from New York City that day, after many hours' delays, and he was headed for his friend's house right from the store.

Although gift giving forges bonds with others and in that sense is a highly social activity, giving a gift is also highly individual, in that gifts are intended for specific individuals to express something about their unique relationship with the giver. Suggesting that children share runs counter to the individualism that is so powerfully hegemonic in our culture.

Equating the worth of the gift with the worth of the recipient helps to explain some instances of extreme overconsumption I witnessed at the two stores. At the Toy Warehouse, one white woman in her thirties came to my register with a cart full of "boys' toys" (easily recognizable as coming from the "Boys' Town" section of the store). I said that this was for some lucky kid, and she said they were for her son's birthday that weekend. She explained that a lot of his friends were out of town for the weekend (it was the Fourth of July) and they weren't going to be able to attend his birthday party. She was worried he wouldn't get enough presents. This was her second time through the store, she told me; she was getting him more to ensure that he had a happy birthday.

The Toy Warehouse encouraged the view that children should be showered with presents on their birthdays. An entire section of the store was devoted to birthday party decorations and accessories, such as piñatas and "party bags"(colorful paper bags that cost $2 for a pack of three) that were supposed to be filled with special "party favor" toys for the birthday guests. On a child's birthday, the store provided free helium-filled balloons, and the staff gathered around, sang "Happy Birthday," and posed for a Polaroid picture around the child.

In my experience, only middle-class children (and the children of the employees) took advantage of these services. The store was much less hospitable to the children from poor families. This was because poor people were assumed to be thieves, not paying consumers. They came under greater surveillance than middle-class people while in the store. Not surprisingly, they were caught stealing more often. In some cases, children were unwitting accomplices in this, as when one woman was caught stuffing merchandise under her child in the stroller. Using a child as a front taught another lesson in consumerism, but it's not clear whether it was overt or hidden.

Poor kids often hung out in and around the Toy Warehouse without adult supervision. Sometimes children came in groups, just wanting to hang out, and I would feel sorry for them because they probably had no place else to go. The norm of service did not apply in their case. They got shooed out if they were not buying.

The neighborhoods surrounding the Toy Warehouse were impoverished and lacked park space. This mall of big box stores was one of the only destinations for the kids in the neighborhood, but it was not a friendly place for them. The land was private property, not public space, so the freedom to pass through and loiter was restricted. There were no park benches or patches of grass to sit on, no meandering sidewalks, no trees to climb, no street life (aside from one hot dog stand set up in the middle of the parking lot). Kids were drawn inside the store where pleasures abounded, but without their paying parents they were not welcomed.

Most of the children I saw on their own were boys, although occasionally groups of girls would wander into the store. I recorded this instance in my field notes:

> A group of three African American girls around age nine to eleven came up to my register to ask how much some candy cost (which they couldn't afford so they didn't buy). I offered them stickers, little promotional badges with the company

logo, which they really liked. It was a slow day, hardly any customers at the registers. One of the girls asked me if I had a rubber band. She had been braiding another one's hair and needed to tie it off. I managed to scrounge one up and they were just delighted. So they were kind of hanging out in front of my register, sitting on the counter, not being obnoxious, just talking and laughing. Then a customer came up and I had to say, I have a customer now. They looked a little anxious and scampered out of the store.

Although I felt bad about sending them away, I reinforced the lesson that receiving positive attention from adults is contingent on being able to buy.

The video game department was the only place in the store where kids were allowed to loiter without spending money. This part of the store was cordoned off from the rest, and customers had to pass through an electronic security gate to enter and exit. Three video monitors were set up for customers to play PlayStation and Dreamworks games, and they went nonstop, so it felt like being in an arcade. Kids played the videos together and often made a lot of noise. My supervisor, nineteen-year-old Mustafa, instructed me to tell the kids that their time was up and they had to leave if they got too loud or swore. Many spent the whole day in the store. They checked out the new games and played them for free, but it was in the context of others' ownership. Everyone around was buying the equipment they were using.

Occasionally poor kids did pay with their own money, but this typically would happen only when they were unaccompanied by adults. On one occasion, a young African American boy, around nine years old, came to the electronics department to buy several expensive videos. He looked dirty and a little scared to me. To pay for the video he reached in his pocket and pulled out a wadded-up $100 bill and several $20s. I was astonished, as were my co-workers when I told them about it. When I gave him his change he clutched it in his hand and turned to walk away. I told him to put it in his pocket before he left the register (I often told kids to do this), fearful that a child with this much cash in his hand would be an easy target for thieves.

Many of the video games that I sold seemed violent to me. The store relied on an industry rating system to indicate their suitability for different age groups. The most violent ones, rated "A" for "Adults Only" by the Entertainment Software Rating Board, were not sold in the store, but we did sell many "M," or mature, videos to anyone over sixteen. The video set up directly in front of my cash register featured two kickboxers, a black man and a white man. Players controlled the kicks and punches. Some of the kids playing or watching the game talked about the characters in racist ways. Almost all the kids were African American; occasionally a group of Asian American boys would come in and take over one of the videos. I didn't see white boys hanging out in this section. If they came in they were with their parents, they knew exactly what they wanted, their parents paid for it, and they got out in a hurry.

Middle-class parents and their children would rarely linger and loiter in the Toy Warehouse, despite the efforts of the store to make it welcoming to them. Kids from the neighborhood apparently made middle-class parents very nervous. Once, while I was in my car on break, I saw two African American boys on bicycles (about fifteen and ten). They were riding around the cars and asking shoppers (mostly the children) what they had gotten and trying to engage them in conversation. I saw them ask a nine-year-old white boy what kind of Game Boy he had gotten as his mom shuffled him into their minivan. Within minutes, two police cars arrived. The officers talked to the boys on bikes, who then went away. The plainclothes security guard came out of the store afterwards and talked to the officers; he later told me that he had called them to complain about the boys. The store wanted to make itself more welcoming to middle-class shoppers; getting rid of neighborhood kids was part of this strategy.

Diamond Toys, on the other hand, extended a welcoming aura to middle-class families. It was a tourist destination that many middle-class adults treated like a hands-on children's museum. They would typically take their children through the store section by section, encouraging them to inspect and admire the toys, pointing out those they remembered from their youth. I never observed this in the Toy Warehouse, which seemed much more child dominated.

The difference was remarkable because the merchandise was virtually identical in the two stores. Diamond Toys maintained a popular impression that they sold only "quality" toys, but really they sold the same toys at higher prices. Some extremely high-priced items were Diamond "exclusives," such as Barbie dolls dressed in designer gowns (which cost as much as $700) and signature luggage imprinted with the company logo ($500 for a single suitcase), but we rarely sold those items, and when we did they were purchased by adult collectors unaccompanied by children. The store did offer special services unavailable at the Toy Warehouse. We would, for example, deliver toys to downtown hotels for free, provide free gift wrapping, ship toys to any destination, or keep parcels in the back room for later pickup after a day of shopping. These services added to the store's image of providing an upper-class shopping experience.

Many of the middle-class shoppers at Diamond Toys were tourists. I observed several instances when children with their parents were allowed to select one small toy as a souvenir of their trip to the store, usually with a cap on the price and the size. These families seemed to treat Diamond Toys as the equivalent of Disneyland. The presence of the exotic, high-priced toys somehow trumped the more plentiful and familiar toys made by Fisher-Price and Mattel, making the store seem special and inspiring reverence and awe. Even though few people bought them, the special toys transformed shopping into a sanctified experience, akin to religious worship and celebration.

Dorothy, my manager at Diamond Toys, instructed me to keep a close watch on any unaccompanied children in the store, but I rarely encountered any. Once a large group of twelve- to thirteen-year-olds entered my section; I later found out that they were on a school field trip into the city and that their teachers were letting them stop in for a bit of shopping before a Tennessee Williams play they were scheduled to see. Dorothy made me get rid of them.

Rarely did I encounter any minority youth in the store who were unaccompanied by adults. I didn't realize this until one day when Chandrika, the eighteen-year-old African American gift wrapper, told me that she thought she saw one of her friends in the store. We weren't allowed to leave our section, so she asked the plainclothes security guard to look around and see if there was a black guy in the store. I asked her about this. Was it really so uncommon for an African American teenager to be in the store that one black person would be so readily apparent? She assured me that a young black man would definitely stand out at Diamond Toys.

SHOPPING FOR IDENTITY

By far, most of the customers at Diamond Toys were adults shopping unaccompanied by children. As I've already noted, the Toy Warehouse was child dominated, while Diamond Toys was adult dominated. Adults didn't come with a list of what children wanted; more typically they bought what *they* wanted. Ellen Seiter (1993, 193) argues that parents and grandparents communicate their values to their children through the toys they buy for them. The toys express their aspirations—educational, class, and status goals—which often conflict with children's desires. At places like the Toy Warehouse, children determined purchases. At Diamond Toys, adults were freer to express their values without having to negotiate with children. They often relied instead on nostalgic images of their own childhoods or on the "expert" advice of the service workers to help them select the best toys for children.

Toys for these well-to-do adult customers can be seen as promoting an approach to child rearing that Annette Lareau (2003) has termed "concerted cultivation." Lareau defines this middle-class cultural logic as "a deliberate and sustained effort to stimulate children's development and to cultivate their cognitive and social skills" (238). Under this regime, playtime is perceived as an opportunity for children to acquire talents and dispositions valued by adults. While children's opinions about their leisure time are solicited, and sometimes trump adults' decisions, this approach is ultimately adult dominated: children's playtime is constantly monitored and assessed for its role in encouraging the development of coveted personality attributes and skills.

"Concerted cultivation" contrasts with the approach to child rearing that Lareau (2003) found in poor and working-class families. There, segregation between adults' and children's worlds is more stark, with adults giving children (especially boys) freer range to pursue their own interests apart from their guidance and supervision. Lareau labels this approach the "accomplishment of natural growth." Toys seem less important to this child-rearing strategy. Of course, poor families buy fewer toys for their children than rich families buy for theirs: Lareau notes in her ethnography that birthdays and Christmas are not celebrated with presents in some poor families (141). But when they do buy toys, poor and working-class parents are apparently more willing to select toys that have no higher educational or cultural value, just the value of the joy they can bring to children.

"Concerted cultivation" was very much in evidence in the purchases of wealthy grandparents shopping at Diamond Toys, who typically selected educational toys. Books were a popular choice, especially those that grandparents recalled as personal favorites from their own childhoods. One grandmother boasted to a friend accompanying her that she bought only books for her grandchildren, who lived in another town. She told me that she would tape-record herself reading the book so that the child could follow along and vicariously experience the pleasure of being read to by Grandma.

Computerized "self-reading" books were first introduced during the season I was working at Diamond Toys. These electronic books come equipped with a stylus that the child can sweep over the text and a computerized voice will "read" the words. Other versions come with LCD pads and pens to allow children to practice their writing and spelling. These items were very popular with parents and grandparents. I never saw a child pick one out.

Computerized instructional toys are intended to be parental replacements, an explicit theme in their marketing (Pugh 2001). Their popularity no doubt reflects the time pressures confronted by many working parents today. Between juggling work and home care responsibilities, parents have very little time and energy left over to play with their kids and teach them to read and write. Buying these expensive toys is a way to ensure their children don't fall behind and to put playtime to productive, if solitary, use.

Expensive toys compensate children in another way. Arlie Hochschild (1997), in writing about the time bind of working parents, notices that many adults try to assuage their sense of guilt toward their children with "time deficit paybacks." They make up for the time not spent with their kids by buying them special treats. At Diamond Toys I would sometimes witness parents looking for appropriate payback gifts for their kids. The classic instance was a parent on a business trip buying something to take to the kids back home, but toys were also purchased to compensate children for the long hours that parents spent in the office. In the following example from my field notes, a mother told me she needed to buy something for her kids because she had been working too many long hours and not paying enough attention to them.

> A white woman of about forty came into the store about 7:00 P.M. looking for small gifts for her children. She came up to me and told me that she hadn't had much time to spend with them and she was feeling guilty about that. She wanted to

buy the two-year-old a cardboard book, and in a rushed tone asked me where they were. (I was sitting on the floor cleaning up a display that had been recently knocked down by shoppers.) I got up and showed her the section. She wanted to know if this was all we had. I said it was most of it; other bits might be scattered around the store. She said she already had most of these titles. I pointed out a few that I thought were new and she started looking at them (no one ever says thank you). I said I would leave her to it, then, and went back to my straightening. Several minutes later she came up to me and said that she needed to check out right away, she was in a hurry, could I do that for her. I said, "Certainly," and walked straight to my register and typed in my cashier code. In the meantime she was waylaid by another display and spent several minutes deciding that maybe she needed to buy a video as well. I was waiting at my register for her to decide. She eventually came up with two "Spot the Dog" videos and asked me which I thought was better. I said I hadn't seen them. She decided not to get them. I rang up her purchase, which was a cardboard book, another book, and a Hello Kitty pencil case. She probably spent about a half hour in my section.

Adults use gifts of toys to reassure children that they are loved even when the adults can't spend time with them. But I couldn't help but think that in this instance the thirty minutes that the mother spent shopping would be better spent hanging out with her kids.

Juliet Schor (2005, 2004) contends that one reason why parents may be spending more hours at work is to purchase more toys for children. She cites research showing that toy expenditures rise by $2.59 for every additional work hour of mothers and $1.26 for fathers. According to Schor (2005, 302), this research indicates that "mothers who worked longer hours did more discretionary spending on their children (controlling for income). Conversely, mothers who spent more time with their children spent less on them."

Of course, this isn't a one-way street. Schor hypothesizes that parents' time deficit paybacks may be demanded by their children. Increasingly, advertising-saturated mass media are replacing adult supervision during after-school hours. As they watch more TV, kids are developing more consumer demands from all the advertisements directed at them. Evidently, many children want their parents to work longer hours to pay for their burgeoning consumer desires (Schor 2005, 302).

In addition to buying nostalgia toys and educational toys, adults selected toys for children that represented their sense of the child's identity. Sometimes this was highly individual, as when one couple came in looking for the Olivia stuffed pig because that was their daughter's name. But more commonly, toys were chosen to represent the race and gender of the child.

Racial/ethnic identity was the one of the most prominent features of personal identity reproduced in adults' selection of toys. The race of the doll or action figure had to "match" the race of the child. On one occasion at the Toy Warehouse, a white mother was buying a dozen different Barbie dolls (the $6 kind) as party favors for her daughter's birthday party. These Barbies came in every skin color, but she selected only white ones, albeit with different hair colors, chosen to match the hair colors of her daughter's friends. (She also bought a dozen identical Barbie outfits to give along with the dolls.) It was exceptional for a white person to buy any doll that wasn't white. One time I helped the white grandparents of an adopted girl from China search for and select a baby doll with Asian features. (They explained their unusual choice to me.) In my experience, only African Americans bought African American dolls, but they sometimes bought white dolls too. White dolls were popular with all racial/ethnic groups, especially celebrity dolls, like the Mary-Kate and Ashley dolls I described above. Many of the toys I sold were tie-ins to television programs, such as *Spongebob Squarepants*, *Madeline*, *Clifford the Dog*, and *Bob the Builder*. They only came in one "race"—usually white—so there was never an option.

The racial/ethnic identity of toys was rarely contested. One time a white couple came in to Diamond Toys and asked me what to get for a three- to four-year-old boy. This kind of question was very common; customers would always specify age and gender when asking for advice. We were instructed in our training never to gender-type toys for children. My manager told us that she hated Barbie growing up, so we shouldn't force gender stereotypes on children. Instead, we were supposed to ask the customer to describe the child's tastes and interests. I tried doing this at first, but it quickly became absurd because very young children don't have any tastes or interests. Moreover, adults who specified the gender of a child treated me as if I were stupid if I needed additional information about their tastes ("You know, a typical twelve-year-old girl"). Thus I gave up and succumbed to gender stereotyping. I suggested to this couple that they might consider buying Bob the Builder, since I had overheard a coworker making this recommendation. The woman laughed and said, "No tools—we're Jewish!" She explained that no one in the family knew how to fix anything or could even pick up a tool. I said maybe it would be handy if someone in the family learned to use tools. She reconsidered and decided it would be funny to purchase a Bob the Builder.

Adults clearly did not want to encourage random qualities in children. Toys for very young children were often selected to reproduce the parents' identity. On one occasion at Diamond Toys, I assisted an adult in purchasing a pewter golf club the size of a rattle to give to a newborn whose mother loved golfing. Gifts could also reflect the adult's fantasies of what the child's identity should be. This helps to make sense of the veritable obsession with gender in toy stores. Gendered toys represent "hegemonic masculinity" and "emphasized femininity"—not what real men and women are but stereotypical, dichotomized traits that are venerated as social ideals (Connell 1995). Thus Barbie is a shapely fashion model, GI Joe is a rapacious fighter. It doesn't matter that few adults embody these cultural ideals; they exist in the world of fantasy, and adults reproduce that fantasy of a perfectly gender-differentiated world in their selection of toys.

The following incident from Diamond Toys illustrates this important function of gendered toys.

White grandparents were in the store looking for tricycles for their two-year-old twin granddaughters (who weren't there with them). I showed them a little trike that's popular and they weren't that interested, so I pointed out the elaborate dump trucks and tractors that we kept in a display on the valence. The grandmother said, "Oh, no, they're girls!" The grandfather accused her of being sexist. She smiled but then got defensive. She told me that her daughter (the girls' mother) was a surgeon in a medical specialty unusual for women but that she was going to buy girl toys for her grand-daughters. They wanted recommendations, so I showed them around, explaining what they would find in the various sections of the store. The grandfather seemed interested in the trains and Bob the Builder (whose sidekick, Wendy, is a girl), but the grandmother said no. If the girls get a brother next, she said, they can play with his toys. But for now she was buying only girl toys.

From adults' perspective, toys can magically compensate for any deviations of a child's parents from idealized gender. Giving a gender-typed toy, they seem to hope, will allow the child to experience the pleasures of gender and pick up some lessons on proper stereotypical behavior. Of course, what a child does with a toy is not so easily determined. Subverting adults' intentions seems to be in the very nature of children's play. As many artists and cultural theorists have argued, even Barbie has a variety of meanings (Lord 1994; McDonough 1999; Rand 1995). Nevertheless, adults often insist on buying toys that represent ideal qualities they want to see reproduced in children's fantasies.

In another example of using toys as a form of gender compensation, an African American woman shopping at Diamond Toys was looking for a Barbie doll for a child she met through a charitable organization. I showed her the ones I liked (the "Generation Girls"), but in the end she decided to pick an African American Barbie in a nursery setting, complete with a little baby and crib. She said since the girl didn't have a mother it would be a nice thing to have a loving maternal setting like this, and I agreed.

I amazed myself by agreeing with her. I live in a world of gender sociologists, where resistance to gender is common and expected. But over time, working in the toy stores, I found my personal resistance weakening. Toy stores were so gender differentiated, as were children's (and adults') desires, that resistance seemed futile. No one ever tried to subvert gender at the Toy Warehouse, which was explicitly divided into "Girls' Town" and "Boys' Town." Even at Diamond Toys, where some of the managers were devoted to challenging gender assumptions, resistance seemed pointless. I confronted Henry, one of the more subversive managers, about this. I had made an offhand comment to him about putting the "boy bears" on the shelf, and he said, "Don't make that assumption!" I said that I didn't, but look at the merchandise: in the infant area, half of the wall was pink and the other half was blue, and the same things were in the two areas in the different colors. Some were explicitly marked by gender, such as the identical pillows inscribed with either "Thank heaven for little girls" or "Little boy blue." Henry shrugged and had to agree with me: the store was very gendered despite (some of) the workers' views.

I was surprised at how rarely gender was contested in toy stores. In three hundred hours of toy selling, I witnessed it only twice. The first time involved a grandmother buying a Barbie substitute for her granddaughter. Here are my field notes:

> A white grandmother (in her sixties) with two younger
> friends (in their fifties) came up and asked me if we had "Get
> Real Girls." These are the slightly larger than Barbie-sized
> dolls that are more like GI Joe. They are not sexy, they are
> tough, and they have joints at their wrists, ankles, etc. They
> come in action sets, dressed for example to go snowboarding,
> or play basketball, or go camping. The grandmother really

liked the dolls, and she bought one for her granddaughter who was ten. She asked me if these were popular, and I said frankly that I had never seen girls look at them in the store; they all wanted Barbie. The grandmother said she didn't like Barbie, but these were wonderful, so she was getting one anyway. She was a bit uncertain, though, because of my comment. There was a ten-year-old white girl nearby with her father who was carefully selecting a Barbie (she had been studying her choices for over fifteen minutes, much to the patient bemusement of her father). I suggested that we ask that girl what she thought about the Get Real Girl. We showed it to her and she scowled at it. She didn't say anything; her expression said it all. The grandmother was undeterred in her decision, but she decided that her granddaughter could return it if she wanted to for something else. But she wanted me to write on the receipt that she couldn't return it for a Barbie! We laughed about that.

The Get Real Girl is gendered, but she represents an alternative to the emphasized femininity of Barbie. The grandmother was doing her part to undermine conventional gender expectations in her granddaughter, a gesture she knew was futile but was committed to nonetheless.

The only other instance of gender resistance that I witnessed didn't turn out to be about resistance at all. This happened when I was working in the infant section of Diamond Toys.

A white grandmother (around sixty-five) was buying a stuffed animal for her newest grandchild. She asked me if I could help her find one with a wind-up music box inside that played classical music. She settled on a light yellow stuffed cat. When she picked out the cat she mentioned that it was a "nice, gender-neutral" choice. Later when she was paying I mentioned her comment and said it was unusual for people to seek out gender-neutral choices. She said it was because she didn't like any of the blue ones on display and she couldn't give the child something pink because his father would have a fit, and that was why gender neutral was OK. In other words, she didn't seek out a gender-neutral toy; it was only the second-best option. But she did tell me that she had worn only pants when she was growing up because she didn't like girls' clothes.

Adults' personal experiences of gender do not seem to affect their choices of toys for girls and boys. Even if they don't conform, or didn't conform in their youth, many want and expect children to have the opportunity to experience conventional gender socialization. In this way, they can share an idealized gender as part of their fantasy life.

SADOMASOCHISM IN THE TOY STORE

Any discussion of parents and children in toy stores would be incomplete without an analysis of the frequent battles between them. Emotions were raw in the toy store. A day wouldn't go by without several children throwing tantrums and shrieking uncontrollably. My impression was that many adults shopped alone at Diamond Toys to avoid the inevitable conflicts with their children over expensive goods. In the Toy Warehouse, on the other hand, crying, screaming children were as common as deliriously happy ones.

Over time I began to understand this constant fighting as enactments of sadomasochism in the parent-child relationship. I use the term *sadomasochism* to characterize a psychological response to ambivalence in intimate relationships.[3] *Ambivalence* refers to the contradictory feelings of love and hate that arise in situations of high dependency. In Freud's work, the quintessential experience of ambivalence is the child's relationship to its parents, but it is a likely reaction to any dependent relationship that a person feels unable to leave. These feelings are often expressed through the mechanism of splitting, which essentially means dividing up the world into "good guys" and "bad guys." The best-known example of this is the Oedipus complex, in which the boy embraces his love for his mother and violently repudiates his father. Although childhood is an extreme case, Freudians argue that intense feelings of ambivalence, often accompanied by the defense mechanism of splitting, are likely to arise in any relationship where people are not free to leave for any number of reasons, including political, ideological, and emotional ones (Smelser 1998).

Ambivalence and splitting also occur between adults, resulting in a sadomasochistic dynamic, which some gender scholars, including Jessica Benjamin (1988), have described as typical of heterosexual relationships. In the classic sadomasochistic pairing, one partner (the sadist) is considered by both to be stronger, smarter, or somehow more talented, gifted, and lovable than the other. The person in the masochistic position is deemed weaker, dependent, and less worthy than the sadist. The masochist longs for the love of the stronger, more deserving and worthy sadist and is willing to do anything to obtain that love. The sadist grants that love only sparingly, if at all, because the masochist isn't considered deserving of recognition, only domination.

Jessica Benjamin links this sadomasochistic dynamic to gender domination and contrasts it with the ideal of "mutual recognition." This happens when both partners recognize their interdependence and are willing to accept each other's merits as well as each other's flaws. Benjamin writes that to recognize another is to "affirm, validate, accept, tolerate, appreciate, and love" the other person (15–16).

The toy store seems designed to promote sadomasochism instead of mutual recognition. Giant toy stores, like the ones where I worked, are like drug dens for kids. Everything is designed to titillate and appeal to the child's most base desires. Kids are overwhelmed by the temptations around them, and many can't control their excitement. But adults stand between children and the gratification of their desires, and this inevitably draws out ambivalent feelings. Thus, not surprisingly, every day during my fieldwork I witnessed a child loudly professing profound love and profound hatred toward an adult.

Of course, parents also expressed ambivalence in the toy store. Parents would often torture children in the store. What often began as a reward or special treat for children turned into an opportunity to discipline and punish them. This is the classic sadomasochistic scenario. Here is one example:

> An Asian American mother was shopping with three kids, all under ten, with the youngest boy about five. The mom was buying an expensive video game for the older kids. While she was dealing with the transaction, the five-year-old boy wandered over to the rack of hand-held video games. He picked one up and took it over to his mother, with very hopeful eyes, asking her, "Please, can I have it?" She didn't say no right away; she just continued with her transaction, which gave the boy a little bit of hope. Then he tried to put it on the counter

and she said, "No," and the kid started to whine. She told him to put it back on the rack. He did halfheartedly and began sobbing. The mom and the other kids moved to exit the store, but the little kid stayed back looking at the toy, crying and eventually shrieking. The mom had to take his hand and drag him out of the store.

In my experience, children would often cry and threaten to escalate into a tantrum if they didn't get what they wanted. The parent would either back down and buy the toy or stand his or her ground. I often witnessed parents who tried to turn disappointment into a lesson in delayed gratification ("If only you had saved your money . . . " or "If you are good, maybe Santa will bring it for Christmas"). The child either accepted this view of himself or herself as not good enough or rebelled and caused a scene. At that point, most parents absolutely refused to back down and it was all-out war. From the parent's point of view, the "bad" child was now undeserving of the love symbolized by the toy purchase (in contrast, perhaps, to the "good" child in the above example who was receiving the expensive video game).[4]

In some instances parents broke down and the sadomasochism of the toy store was reversed, with the child as sadist. Here is one example:

A twelve-year-old white boy was with his mother, who was buying over $150 worth of toys for him, mostly Legos. She asked me if we had Game Boy Advance in stock, and I said we were sold out. The kid got angry at his mother, blaming her for there not being any. He walked off, looking as if he was going to cry, he was so upset. She told me that it probably was her fault because she had put off getting one for so long since they were so expensive and she didn't really want to buy him one. I mentioned to her that kids didn't really understand how much things cost. We talked about kids' allowances. She said she didn't give her kid an allowance but she had a "point system" with her child, that he got a certain number for doing chores around the house, plus he got points for getting good grades. These points were then converted to cash. As we were talking, her angry and sulking twelve-year-old had roamed off into the store looking for other things that his mother could buy for him to compensate for his loss of the Game Boy.

In this case, the mother was desperately seeking recognition from her son by catering to his needs and desires without concern for her own; she felt guilty for acting on her own desire to save money. He was clearly the worthier one in this sadomasochistic pairing.

These incidents also reflect features of the "concerted cultivation" approach to child rearing described by Annette Lareau. This middle-class style of upbringing empowers children to voice their preferences, with the ultimate aim of encouraging them to recognize and develop sophisticated tastes. One of the downsides of the strategy is that it tends to produce whiny, combative children. Lareau (2003, 241) observes that, in her study, "middle-class children, Black and white, . . . squabbled and fought with their siblings and talked back to their parents. These behaviors were simply not tolerated in working-class and poor families, Black or white."

Middle-class parents were often dismayed or even embarrassed by their children's behavior. They expected their children to limit or curb their desires, not to act greedily. From the middle-class parent's perspective, buying a toy is a special "treat" to express their love and to reward the child for good behavior (Kline 1993). But by bringing children to a store that surrounds them with temptation, parents are sending children a mixed message: it is good to control your desires, *and* since you have been good, or since you are loved, you may select something from the garden of earthly delights. Self-control is rewarded with splurging. It shouldn't be surprising, then, if children think that being really good (or really loved) merits a really good—that is, expensive—toy, or at least a lot of toys. This idea, that owning expensive toys or a large number of toys marks someone as a more deserving person, legitimizes economic inequality by framing it as a reflection of self-worth.[5]

Iulie Aslaksen (2002) argues that the gift can also be a reflection of the worth of the giver. She speculates that extreme generosity may be common among those who fear they are not loved. "Giving too much," she writes, "can be a way to try to make other people show love and appreciation, thus inducing others to behave in a way that alleviates one's own fear for lack of love" (128–29). She maintains that women are especially prone to giving too much because of the sexist devaluation of women and the care work they provide. The flip side of this is what she characterizes as the stereotypical masculine tendency to not give enough. Not giving enough reflects too much self-love and not enough of the capacity to relate to others. In the previous incident, the self-effacing mother and the dominant, greedy son replicate this pattern and the gendered underpinnings of hyperconsumerism.

In this final example of sadomasochistic dynamics, the quest for recognition goes back and forth like a seesaw as both parent and child struggle to get what they want from the other:

> An African American mother was walking slowly around the store, and her eight-year-old son came up to her with a plastic-wrapped toy soldier game and begged her for it. She looked down her nose at it, frowned, and didn't say anything. The kid began pleading with her. She took the toy from him and walked slowly over to my register. She said to the kid, "That means you're going to be real good tomorrow." The kid had won and he jumped up triumphantly. But then he was *off!* He started running around the store looking at other possible things to buy, grabbed something almost at random, and brought it to her. She said, "Oh, no way!" She bought the first toy and told me that maybe it would last a week, meaning that the kid would be good for a week if she was lucky. The boy then started playing on the video game set up in the store. After the transaction, the woman wanted to leave and the kid was *not* obeying at all. She yelled at him to get him to leave.

Both the mother and the child longed for the other to be "good" to them—the child wanting toys, the mother wanting respect and obedience. But neither was willing to recognize his or her dependence on the other to achieve these goals. To achieve mutual recognition, it is essential that both parties consider the other's needs and desires as they pursue their own satisfaction and that both recognize their paradoxical dependence on the other to recognize their autonomy.

What would mutual recognition look like in the toy store? Allison Pugh (2003, 11) suggests that a toy can be emblematic of mutual recognition if "the parent 'recognizes' the child in knowing their child so well they know exactly what the child needs and desires, while the child 'recognizes' that the parent got it right, and thus acknowledges the parent's competence, accuracy and love embodied in his or her true knowledge of the child." In contrast, in all of the above examples, the quest for mutual recognition has broken down into domination and subordination. One person tries to force his or her will on the other, refusing to recognize the other's needs, with the result of emotional pain and loss of mutual respect.

Our consumer culture may fuel these sadomasochistic dynamics. The toy store may distort the parent-child relationship and promote the domination and subordination that I witnessed. Most parents probably do not want to spoil their children, but they are encouraged by mass media, advertising, and peer pressure to use money and gifts to symbolize love for their children (and, indeed, for everyone they care about). But when children associate "being good" with getting "points" or receiving toys, love is no longer an end in itself. Thus the plaintive wail in the toy store: "If you really loved me, you would buy it for me."[6]

Part of the allure of consumer culture is its promise that our human needs for love can be met by purchasing goods and services. Children are not the only ones vulnerable to this capitalistic logic. Advertisers try to convince us all that buying their products will make us loved and admired. They assure us that we do not have to sacrifice our desire for independence and narcissistic pleasure to satisfy our needs for dependency and care. This "fantasy of the perfect commodity" can be irresistible. But it is based on a false premise, that human ambivalence can be resolved once and for all.[7] Instead, achieving social recognition through gifts or money may make us more insecure than before, more in need of reassurance that the recognition we get from others is authentic and not superficial and fleeting.

I think that this may be what is happening in the toy store. When parents' affections are expressed primarily through purchases, it seems likely that children will develop fears that they are not loved if they don't receive gifts, leading to compulsive desires for more and more toys—many of which will sit idle on the shelf at home. Similarly, fears that children are good only because they want toys can feed insecurity in adults and lead to compulsions to give more and more. Any attempt at resisting this consumer logic can easily break down into domination and subordination, especially because it takes place in a parent-child relationship characterized by nearly complete economic, social, and psychological dependency. A parent who refuses to buy for a child faces accusations of withholding love, thereby making the child feel unworthy or else compelling the child to demand recognition by throwing a tantrum. In this way, sadomasochism and hyperconsumerism may be flip sides of the same coin.

CONCLUSION

Although we are not "born to shop," most American children learn how to do it at a very early age. Adults teach children consumer skills, including accounting, money management, and comparison shopping. They also teach children that we honor our loved ones by buying them things that reflect our feelings for them. What we buy is determined sometimes by the giver, sometimes by the receiver. The Toy Warehouse catered to the receiving child. Adults often rewarded children for their specialness by letting them select from the cornucopia of riches, but then they were disappointed when the child was too greedy. Diamond Toys catered instead to the giving adult. Many adults were keenly sensitive to the impact of their gifts on children, believing that they were shaping children through their purchases, so they selected toys with purported educational value, nostalgia toys, or toys that reflected idealized qualities they wished to see in the children's identity. Toy shopping was thus part of the child-rearing strategy of concerted cultivation favored by middle-class adults.

There are covert and unintended lessons in the shopping curriculum too, many involving the reproduction of social inequality. Rewarding good behavior with presents bolsters the view that only the "worthy" get rewarded, adding legitimacy to the system of class inequality. The fact that buying toys is mostly women's work that they do out of love (or their own emotional needs for love) reproduces gender differentiation and inequality. And reserving the expensive toy store for adults sends children the message that they cannot be trusted to buy expensive toys because they are not yet capable of making the "right" choices.

Other groups were also excluded from Diamond Toys, most notably minority youth, suggesting that they, too, could not be trusted to make the "right" choices. Unlike the Toy Warehouse, which was an amazing mix of social classes and racial/ethnic groups, Diamond Toys was virtually all white and middle to upper class. Although Diamond Toys cultivated its image as the seller of "exclusive" toys, in fact its exclusivity resided more in the clientele it served (and the staff it employed). This equation of "high-quality" merchandise with a predominantly white and wealthy shopping environment formed part of the hidden curriculum of shopping. It justified economic and racial inequality along the lines suggested by Bourdieu by confirming the view that only rich white people had cultivated tastes and hence that only they had the right to shop there.

In this chapter I have also argued that toy shopping may fuel sadomasochistic dynamics in the adult-child relationship. Inside the toy store, the child's desires are hyperstimulated. Satisfaction seems tantalizingly close, separated by a thin layer of plastic coating. But because the child is completely dependent on the adult to gratify those desires, it is not surprising that many children experience and express intensely ambivalent feelings. In highly public displays, the battle for recognition plays out again and again, with clear winners and losers each time. Toy stores stack the deck against mutual recognition.

Learning to shop is necessary for living in a consumer society. Through our purchases, we acquire the means to survival, express who we are, and establish and maintain social relationships. Thus we have to teach children how to do it. Protecting them from shopping would disadvantage them later in life, denying them access to an important means of public participation. Some may fantasize about a halcyon past when people made things instead of buying them, but that is an extremely idealistic and unreasonable option for most people today. Consumerism is here to stay. But how we practice and organize consumption is a social negotiable. Can we teach our children better shopping values? Can equality, fairness, and humane relationships be practiced inside toy stores? This is a topic I will take up in the final chapter.

6

TOYS AND CITIZENSHIP

"If you're good, maybe Santa will buy that for you."

—MOTHER SHOPPING AT DIAMOND TOYS WITH HER CHILD

In the 1950s, David Riesman (1953) described the transition in America from a producer society to a consumer society. He lamented the result for the American character, which changed from inner directed to outer directed and from disciplined and moral to status seeking and superficial. Today that transformation has reached even deeper into the culture and psyche of Americans. What we buy and how we buy express our intimate longings, family ties, and social and political goals. Hardly any aspect of our culture escapes the logic of consumerism. As the mother quoted above attests, even Santa is a consumer now. Shopping defines our individuality, our group affiliations, and even our national identity.

The connection between consumerism and national identity was brought home to me on one of my last days working at the Toy Warehouse. Two white women came to my register late in the evening. They were buying a massive number of girls' toys, including baby dolls, strollers, Fisher-Price family dolls, doll houses, and baby doll cribs. Their purchases filled over five large bags the size of outdoor trash bags. One of the woman asked me if there was a discount for charitable causes. I explained that we did have institutional sales but that they would need a preapproved purchase order. She said this wasn't like that, that they were buying gifts for two orphan girls. There was a story in that day's newspaper about a program to place Romanian orphans, so I asked if that was what this was, and she said no, but it was something similar. Their group had brought two girls, ages five and six, over from someplace in the former Soviet Union, and both had been adopted. These were gifts to welcome them to America. The women had a great deal of money to spend on the girls, up to $400, they told me. They were amazed that with all they had purchased the total came to only $300. I said something about how this was going to be totally overwhelming to these girls, and one of them paused and said maybe I was right; perhaps what they should do was to give one toy each week. But the other said, "Then they will begin to expect one toy a week and they will be disappointed if they don't get one." I left them to figure that out while I pondered the social, cultural, and psychological implications of their largesse.

Becoming American for these girls would mean becoming consumers. For generations, immigrants have looked to the United States as the land of opportunity and prosperity, characteristics that are a source of national pride for many Americans. But, I thought to myself, where do these boundless riches come from? The vast array of consumer goods in our society, including the inexpensive toys purchased for the orphan girls, were manufactured in the third world, maybe even in the former Soviet Union, maybe even by children. I suspect that the irony of this situation, if anyone noticed it, would only reinforce the sense that these girls were lucky to have made it to America.

Americans spend so much time shopping that we rarely think about its social impact, much less its global consequences. Consumerism forms a ubiquitous backdrop to our daily lives; we could hardly escape the constant pressures and opportunities to buy even if we tried. In my opinion, all of this shopping is not good for our society. As I have argued in this book, consumerism, as it is practiced today, plays a key role in reproducing social inequality. The organization of stores perpetuates inequality through gender, race, and class stratification; the interactions on the shopping floor enact and reproduce the matrix of domination; and the lessons we teach our children about shopping legitimize economic and social inequality. However, these problems are not here to stay. The fact that shopping as a national pastime emerged less than a century ago and the rapid pace of change we are witnessing in its evolution today suggest that, far from being inevitable, the way we shop can be altered.

Changing the social organization of shopping does not mean eliminating shopping altogether, or even necessarily cutting back on the acquisition of consumer goods. In my view, there is nothing inherently evil or even troubling about the drive to acquire commodities. Accumulating more and better things does not signal a growing moral turpitude or cultural decline. Thus I part ways with critics of consumerism who advocate "simplicity" as the cure for our "affluenza." Instead, I celebrate the richness and the transformative power of material things.

I take inspiration for my position from an unlikely source, Karl Marx. Marx is well known for his trenchant criticisms of the social organization of capitalism. Perhaps less well known is the fact that Marx celebrated the human impulse to objectify ourselves through the production of material things. Our ability to understand our needs and to imagine innovative ways to fulfill them was to Marx the one outstanding characteristic of humanity that distinguished us from other animals. In a famous passage in *Capital*, he describes the differences between spiders and bees on the one hand and humans on the other, emphasizing our species' ability to transform the natural world and ultimately ourselves through our productive activity: "A spider constructs operations that resemble those of a weaver, and a bee puts to shame many an architect in the construction of her cells. But what distinguishes the worst architect from the best of bees is this, that the architect raises his structure in imagination before he erects it in reality. At the end of every labor-process, we get a result that already existed in the imagination of the laborer at its commencement" (Marx, 1978 [1867], 344–45).

This capacity to use our creative powers of imagination to transform the objective and external world (in this case by weaving a cloth or constructing a building) is what makes us distinctively human. Marx argues that we have been alienated from this capacity due to the capitalist organization of production. In his view, capitalism prevents workers from realizing their creative powers because they are forced to manufacture commodities they have no hand in designing or choosing. But the good news is that our species' capacity for self-objectification makes possible the quest for a better, more equitable and fair social order. Because we can imagine a better world, we can use our human potential to transform our current social and economic arrangements.

Of course, Marx was talking about production, not consumption, when he pondered our capacity for objectification and social transformation. But today, very few of us are involved in producing the commodities we use to express ourselves; we now buy to satisfy our creative needs. Today, the social relations of consumption, in addition to the social relations of production analyzed by Marx, perpetuate social inequalities and prevent the establishment of a more just social order. The goal, then, is to figure out how consumption might be reorganized to promote social justice and not to create and exacerbate inequality and hardship.

History can provide us with some clues to how consumption might be organized differently. Lizabeth Cohen (2003) argues that two models of consumer citizenship vied for dominance in twentieth-century America. One model, which she calls the "purchaser citizen," has been favored by business interests, theorized by Keynesian economists, and promoted by conservative politicians. Underpinning this view is the belief that the country's best interests are served by individuals pursuing their selfish desires in the unregulated marketplace. Producers should be unfettered by government regulations, they believe, and consumers should be encouraged to buy whatever they want to—as long as they buy a lot. Government should have a role in cultivating consumer desires to stimulate production but only a limited role in regulating what we buy (caveat emptor: let the buyer beware). The theory is that more buying and selling will result in greater prosperity and happiness for all.

If this sounds familiar, that is because it is the hegemonic view of consumerism today, undergirded by the most powerful social, cultural, and political institutions. When the government urged us to "Shop for America" in the months following the September 11 terrorist attacks, the model of the "purchaser citizen" was being evoked to stave off economic recession. America would be "open for business," as one government slogan insisted, despite the ongoing international crisis.

Cohen (2003) counterposes the "purchaser citizen" to a second model of consumer citizenship, which she calls the "citizen consumer." This model of citizenship imagines an educated and engaged shopper interacting with a socially responsible producer. Government has a critical role to play in regulating the marketplace in order to protect the safety and well-being of both workers and consumers. The state, not the market, should determine and enforce standards for the healthfulness, the quality, and, if necessary, the price of goods. Social prosperity is guaranteed through commitment to satisfying the general welfare, not through cultivating the selfish interest of individuals. Consequently, shoppers may be called upon to sacrifice by delaying consumption or spending for things that may not benefit them directly or immediately, such as schools, hospitals, and public transportation systems.

This second model of consumer citizenship has been around for over a hundred years. It was articulated during the progressive movement of the 1920s and 1930s, the civil rights movement of the 1960s, and, most recently, the environmental and labor movements that have challenged the increasing power and devastation wrought by international corporations around the globe. But this model of the citizen consumer has never been hegemonic in the United States, with the exception of one short period around World War II. In that era Americans were urged by their country to "shop for America" but in a way that promoted the general good and not immediate selfish gratification. The government encouraged and expected consumers to ration key commodities, to carpool or take public transportation, to buy war bonds, to refuse the temptations of the black market, and to recycle scarce resources. Many shoppers came to understand the larger implications of what they purchased and where they shopped. They

made consumer choices that reflected their sense of social responsibility and commitment to shared social values. They expressed their values not only through selecting what goods to buy
but also in public discussions over defining their needs and how
these should be met.

In this model of the citizen consumer Cohen sees hope for
reinvigorating democracy and social justice. Her book begins and
ends with the question of how consumption can deliver not only
prosperity but also more social egalitarianism, more democratic
participation, and more political freedom. She argues that the
model of consumer citizenship that "won"—the purchaser consumer—seems to undermine these goals. The ideal of the citizen
consumer that prevailed in the 1930s and 1940s seems more compatible with these general aims.

What would the model of the "consumer citizen" look like in
the toy store? How might the retail industry be transformed to
promote this ideal of citizenship and social responsibility? There
is no single answer to this question, but several approaches may
contribute to better, less alienating shopping conditions for all.

SHOP LOCALLY

Many critics of American consumerism maintain that the local,
"mom and pop" retail establishment is socially, morally, and aesthetically superior to the big box franchise store. Large corporate
"palaces of consumption" are faulted for their homogeneity, their
sterility, and the banality of their design in contrast to locally
owned shops, which are celebrated as more humane places where
individuality and "quirky and pleasing novelty" can be experienced (Kellner 1999, 201). Neighborhood toy stores still exist in

many communities, although their numbers are dwindling. Is this where the citizen consumer would shop?

Curious about the social conditions of retail work in these establishments, I applied to work at one that was located in the same metropolitan area as the Toy Warehouse and Diamond Toys. This store, which I call "Tomatoes," was a small, family-owned business in an upper-middle-class neighborhood located on a busy street with lots of pedestrian traffic. It had been in the neighborhood for twenty-five years, owned by the same family. It sold an offbeat assortment of toys, including many traditional items, like kites and wooden blocks, and a variety of toys I would label "politically correct." It didn't carry Barbie, for example, but it did have "Get Real Girls," the female action figures that look like GI Joe's sisters. I laughed when I saw a pack of plastic "multicultural" food, including spaghetti, sushi, a taco, and a bagel. Then I noticed that these items were marked "Made in China."

Working conditions at the store seemed very relaxed compared to what I had experienced. The owner was dressed in shorts and a Hawaiian shirt, and the workers' dress reflected the sartorial choices of punk college students, including weirdly dyed hair, piercings, and tattoos. They didn't wear uniforms; far from it. One clerk wore her T-shirt hiked up in a knot in the front and stuffed under her bra in the back. There seemed to be very friendly and informal relationships between the workers and the owner. While I was waiting for my interview, I witnessed one clerk successfully negotiating for extra time off. Clerks seemed to be on a friendly, first-name basis with several of the customers, most of whom were middle-class white women.

Although I didn't get hired at that store, after several visits I was able to detect social patterns in the store's organization. The owner and the manager were both white men, and all the clerks were young white women. The owner was the only one in the store who was near my age, around forty; everyone else seemed to be in his or her twenties. The job was "flexible" and pay was comparable to what I earned at Diamond Toys. During my interview, I told the owner that I had worked at Diamond Toys, hoping that that experience would enhance my chances for a job, but it made him almost hostile toward me. He said that every time he shopped at Diamond Toys he could never find someone to help him, so that didn't impress him at all. I was surprised, but I didn't say anything. He said he wasn't looking to hire an expert in toys; anyone could learn about the merchandise. He was looking for friendly people, he said, because you can't teach that. He told me that many of the workers were in graduate school, and he asked me if I had plans to go back to school (perplexing because I had put my advanced degrees on my application).

You can never be sure why you don't get offered a job, but my impression is that I wasn't young enough or hip enough to work at Tomatoes. This was the "au pair" equivalent of retail work.[1] Although the working conditions apparently allowed for greater autonomy and self-expression than those of the stores where I worked, race, class, and gender inequality was as much a part of their social organization as in retail work in general.

My experience at Tomatoes made me suspicious of shopping solutions that claim moral superiority for the local neighborhood store. They may play upon our nostalgic longings for a small-town America, but local stores can be just as discriminatory and exclusionary as the big box alternatives. In my experience, the main thing distinguishing the locals from the big boxes is that more educated and wealthy people are likely to shop and to work there. Moreover, the toys they sell are no different from most of those available at the Toy Warehouse or Diamond Toys. They are made in the third world, part of the global economy.

Although the social relations of production and consumption are not drastically different, some argue that shopping locally is better for the environment and for the public coffers. This argument is more compelling. Having the option to walk to a neighborhood store can promote healthy communities, unlike being forced to drive to a big box warehouse. And insofar as the sales tax dollars generated by local businesses stay in inner cities instead of sprawling suburban developments, the social welfare of the community may be enhanced by them.

But in general, the "shop locally" approach is not the solution to the inequalities I've described in this book. The major drawback, in addition to perpetuating social exclusivity, is that this strategy relies on the individual consumer to alter the social relations of consumption. Individual solutions are more adept at promoting guilt than at effecting social change. Although it is always important to do what we can, challenging the social inequality embedded in the retail industry would require changes far beyond the capacity of a single consumer. One shopper cannot change the basic organization of the work. That will require collective action.

The term *collective action* is usually applied to workers and not consumers. But as history shows, organized consumer activism can be as important as workers' unions in supporting equality, justice, and prosperity. Ideally, these two groups—workers and consumers—would combine forces, as they did in the Progressive Era when sociologist Annie Marion MacLean did her fieldwork inside department stores. It is a natural alliance, since all workers are consumers and most consumers are workers. To the extent that worker-consumers can recognize and act on their joint interests, changes in the retail industry are possible.

Below I discuss examples of the kinds of changes that collective and united worker-consumer activism can inspire.

LIVING-WAGE CAMPAIGNS

During the Progressive Era, improving working conditions was a principal demand of the consumer movement (Mayer 1989, 58). Although since then conflicting goals of the consumer and labor movements (for example, lower prices versus higher wages) have led to strains, recent consumer-worker alliances around specific issues have brought about beneficial, albeit limited, reforms. Among these are consumer protests against sweatshops producing celebrity-branded fashion clothing (Cathy Gifford, Nike, Gap), student protests against human rights abuses in the manufacture of apparel with university logos, and children's protests against soccer balls produced with foreign child labor (Clawson 2003).

This consumer organizing on behalf of workers has mostly focused on enhancing the wages and working conditions of manufacturing employees and not service workers, but there are exceptions. For instance, the Justice for Janitors movement in California drew support from taxpayer groups concerned about the public cost of paying for these low-paid workers' use of social welfare services (Rudy 2004). Consumers also supported the UPS strike of 1997; they empathized with the economic plight of the hardworking delivery men and women they encountered every day (Martin 2004). And during the civil rights era, consumers boycotted stores that refused to hire African Americans (Weems

1998). But not since the Progressive Era have retail workers enjoyed widespread popular support. Back then, shoppers who were members of the Consumers' League would purchase goods only from clerks wearing union buttons. Bourgeois women would stage "sip-ins" in department store cafeterias, monopolizing table space for hours over a single cup of tea, in order to protest the working conditions of salesclerks (Cohen 2003). These activists drew the connection between their role as consumers and the social and economic plight of retail workers.

Today that connection has been severed. Many customers do not view retail workers as deserving of higher pay and better working conditions. Some do not even consider them worthy of civility. In my experience, if customers' desires weren't satisfied, some would become threatening—"I will never shop at your store again!"—and even violent. On a day when two of my coworkers failed to show up for work, one man told me I should "fire them" because their absence made him have to wait longer than he felt he should. My African American coworkers were subjected to even harsher abuse, as many white customers treated them with disdain.

Part of the reason for the incivility of shoppers may be the mismatch between the ideal and the reality of the shopping experience today. Toy stores market themselves in their advertisements as places of "fun and discovery" staffed by helpful and friendly workers, but the stores do not provide working conditions to nourish such an environment. The result is frequent disappointment and frustration on both sides. Customers expecting cheerful advice and speedy service often encounter a sales force that is tired, bored, resentful, and apathetic. After working in the toy stores, I find it amazing that any salesclerk cares at all. Most are overworked and underpaid; they are allowed limited discretion and virtually no say in how the store is organized. They don't even control their own hours from week to week unless they have a union to protect them. Not surprisingly, the turnover in retail work is among the highest in the labor force.

Store owners have defended the substandard working conditions in the industry by redefining retail jobs as entry-level employment, not intended to be anyone's final working destination. The successful marketing of "McJobs" as temporary part-time employment for teenagers after school, mothers seeking "pin money," or seniors looking for a chance to get out of the house justifies their low status and pay. Since these workers don't really "need" the money they earn, there is no reason to upgrade their jobs by providing good wages, benefits, vacation leave, or autonomy.

Many economists accept the distinction between "good jobs" and "bad jobs" as a basic feature of a capitalist economy (Levy 1998). "Bad jobs," such as those in retail, give workers a needed economic incentive to invest in the training demanded of higher-level jobs and professions. Others argue that every job should be a "good job." If a job is worth doing, it is worth receiving the pay and recognition of a wage high enough to sustain a reasonable standard of living for the worker.

Living-wage campaigns embody a first step toward the latter goal of eliminating "bad jobs." These campaigns demand not minimum wages but "living" wages for all employees, defined as "enough so that a full-time, year round worker can support a family at the poverty line" (Clawson 2003, 164). The basic goal is to transform all low-level jobs, including retail work in addition to other front-line service and manufacturing work, into "good jobs," paying above-poverty wages and providing sick leave and vacation pay. This is in contrast to current public policy, which guarantees only a poverty-level minimum wage (if that!) and encourages workers in these "bad" jobs to seek retraining for better jobs in order to upgrade their status and pay. In my view, upgrading the proliferating jobs in the service sector through living-wage reforms seems like a better long-range approach to promoting the welfare of economically marginalized workers in this growing sector of the economy.[2]

In addition to living wages, all workers—and not just those in "good jobs"—deserve health care benefits. Loopholes allowing corporations to deny benefits to employees should be closed. Consumers have a role to play in pressing for these changes because they in effect subsidize the below-poverty wages paid by retail establishments. A television exposé of Wal-Mart disclosed that the store teaches managers to help workers apply for welfare benefits. Instead of paying their health care benefits, they pass this cost on to the American public. Consumers may save money at the store, but they pay for it in higher taxes to support the social welfare infrastructure (Social Security, emergency cash assistance, food stamps, Medicare) that retail workers are compelled to use.[3]

Campaigns for living wages have proliferated around the country, and the principle is now enforced in several municipalities. These drives have been led by a variety of people, not all of whom benefit directly from its implementation. Labor, community, and religious groups have all played a part (Clawson 2003).[4] In my view, these efforts may be a better alternative than traditional union organizing, especially for workers at the low end of the pay scale in retail employment. Big box retail stores have been extremely effective in thwarting unionizing efforts among their workers, thanks largely to the high turnover rates they cultivate and the probusiness "right to work" laws they support. Although the goal of the living-wage campaign is modest in comparison to most union demands—to keep all working Americans out of poverty—it represents a critical salvo in the fight to improve the social conditions of retail work for those at the bottom.

RACIAL DIVERSITY

Ideally, consumer citizenship should concern itself with challenging forms of inequality other than the purely economic. As I have argued, the way we shop today promotes race and gender inequality in addition to class inequality. Transforming the retail industry will also require addressing these forms of disadvantage.

Ever since I worked in the toy stores, I have noticed racial diversity (or its absence) wherever I shop. Granted the high degree of residential segregation in this country, it is not surprising that many stores are highly segregated as well. But some retailers build to exclude. The history of suburban malls is a history of intentional racial segregation (Cohen 2003). Even today, so-called desirable retail locations are characterized by limited access. The local malls in my city of Austin have *opposed* public bus service on the grounds that it would encourage undesirable (that is, nonwhite) patronage. In my view, city ordinances should prevent this by refusing to grant retail building permits in areas that are underserved by public transportation.

But geographical access is not enough to ensure racial diversity. Recall that Diamond Toys was located in an urban shopping district. It was right next to the subway and bus lines, yet nearly all of its patrons were white. One way that many stores exude hostility to racial/ethnic minorities is through consumer racial profiling. Like racial profiling in police work, consumer racial profiling refers to detaining, searching, and harassing racial/ethnic minorities at a higher rate than whites, usually because they are suspected of stealing. Jerome Williams and his colleagues refer to the putative violation as "shopping while black" (Williams, Henderson, and Harris 2001). They claim that even though white women in their fifties make up the largest percentage of shoplifters, nonwhite minorities are the most likely to be "profiled" as thieves. Their research on over a hundred stores charged with racial profiling demonstrates the ubiquity of the problem and the difficulty of successful prosecution. Thirty percent of African Americans claim that they have experienced discrimination while shopping, yet few of these cases ever make it to court. The discrepancy is due in part to the difficulty of demonstrating discrimination (was it poor service or discrimination?) and in part to weak laws. Title II of the 1964 Civil Rights Act does prohibit racial discrimination in public accommodation (including hotels and restaurants), but retail establishments are excluded from its scope. (In contrast, the Americans with Disabilities Act does include retail stores.) Furthermore, Title II provides only "injunctive relief," not monetary damage awards, to those who have faced discrimination. This means that establishments found guilty can be forced to alter their practices, but individuals cannot sue for damages, making a guilty verdict a relatively painless outcome for stores that practice consumer racial profiling.

According to Anne-Marie Harris (2003), an 1866 law giving racial/ethnic minorities the right to make and enforce contracts has been deployed more successfully than Title II in consumer racial profiling cases. Under the 1866 law, plaintiffs can take retail establishments to court if they interfere with or undermine their ability to purchase an item, which is technically considered making a contract. But this law, too, is inadequate to deal with the larger problem of "shopping while black." To qualify for damages, consumers still have to prove intentional discrimination on the part of the retailer. This law is also limited in that plaintiffs can win their cases only if they were *denied* services, not if the services they received were inferior or if they were harassed while they were shopping, which is the likelier scenario. Thus, if an individual is subjected to stepped-up surveillance, or if her bags are subjected to search after her purchase is completed, then the law doesn't technically apply. All of this is to say that stricter antidiscrimination laws are needed, and standards for evidence should be relaxed or altered if customers are ever to enjoy legal redress for discrimination in stores.

What would it mean to alter the standards of evidence in consumer racial profiling cases? Here we can take a page out of the sexual harassment policy reforms advocated by legal scholar Vicki Schultz (1998). Schultz argues that the social and cultural context of the organization should be considered when ascertaining the existence of hostile environment complaints of sexual harassment and gender discrimination. Instead of focusing on discrete incidents of harassment, Shultz argues that a "big picture" of the organization's treatment of women is necessary to ascertain discrimination. Applied to the problem of racism in the shopping context, Shultz's approach would require courts to consider questions such as: How diverse is the management? How frequently are racial/ethnic minority workers hired, promoted, and fired? How do the store demographics compare with the region's demographics? How frequently are minorities portrayed in store advertisements? Allowing this sort of evidence into the courtroom might result in more frequent and successful prosecutions of consumer racial profiling.

In their defense, store executives claim that they have no interest in discriminating and that the poor publicity associated with consumer racial profiling cases is expensive (in terms of lost business) and extremely difficult to overcome (Adamson 2000). According to Dan Butler (2004) of the National Retail Federation, some stores have taken drastic measures to prevent it, by, for example, instituting "no stop" rules. This policy prohibits store clerks from detaining any shopper suspected of stealing unless there is irrefutable recorded evidence of the theft (increasingly possible thanks to enhanced digital surveillance in stores). Store employees who make "bad stops"—that is, those who detain shoppers who are not guilty of stealing—are subjected to termination on the spot.

These legal and law enforcement approaches to ending discrimination must be part of any effort to enhance diversity in the shopping experience. But to make stores truly welcoming to a wide variety of customers, the merchandise must appeal to nonwhite consumers. Racial targeting aims to make desirable products and services available to racial/ethnic minorities, unlike racial profiling, which is about denying products and services or offering inferior versions of these. Geraldine Henderson (2004) argues that refusing to stock products for blacks is a form of racial profiling because it sends the message to minority consumers that their business is not wanted. Henderson warns retailers, "If you don't court customers, your customers may take you to court."

What does racial targeting mean in the case of the toy store? As we saw in chapter 5, racial identity is inscribed in many of the toys purchased for children. Including an array of choices that feature racial/ethnic diversity in both the product and the marketing seems critical to providing a welcoming shopping environment for nonwhite consumers. Because these products are often manufactured by nonwhite firms, an added impact can be in supporting minority businesses.

None of these proposed solutions address the problem of racism among shoppers, however. The unfortunate fact is that many white shoppers prefer to shop in segregated environments. James Farrell (2003) points out that, to some extent, consumer racial profiling takes place to please white customers. He writes, "Middle class white Americans often get nervous around groups of young black men, and so store employees and mall security are often more watchful around such young men. When this happens, black people suffer for white people's enjoyment" (152–53).

This racism of shoppers is rarely articulated directly; it is articulated only indirectly, through the choice of where to shop. Farrell points out that many middle-class white parents permit teens and "tweens" to go to the mall on their own to meet with friends and hang out. He writes, "For parents, the mall is an oasis of security in a world of seeming dangers" (102). Racial exclusivity contributes to this sense of the mall as a "safe space" for these white parents. This helps to explain the difficulty that the Toy Warehouse faced in attracting middle-class white customers. The store wanted to provide a welcoming atmosphere to encourage white middle-class mothers to linger and explore, but its meager

efforts were wasted: the racial diversity of the store was not allur-
ing to this group of coveted shoppers.

Racism is also expressed in the choice of how to shop. Many
customers treat store clerks with disdain and condescension, a
problem that is only exacerbated when the store clerk is black or
Latina/o and the shopper is white, as we saw in chapter 4. The
capitalist mantra that "the customer is always right" can prevent
workers from fighting back. Challenging the racism of customers
will require changing this basic premise.

Efforts to undermine shoppers' racism might take another
page out of the book of sexual harassment policy. In some industries, service workers subjected to sexual harassment by customers have been empowered by management to resist this behavior. This is the case with airline flight attendants, who won a
contract that specifically prohibits harassment from passengers.
In some countries where racial and sexual harassment are pro-
hibited under sweeping human rights legislation, it may be easier
to get the word out that hostile and dehumanizing behavior
toward store clerks is not tolerated and can subject customers as
well as employers to litigation (Williams 2002).

GENDER EQUALITY

Like every industry in the country, retail is male dominated. Even
though most salesclerks are women, men outnumber women as
CEOs, board members, store directors, and managers. At the
stores where I worked and where I interviewed for jobs, all the directors were white men. Clearly there are gender as well as racial
barriers to making it to the top of this industry.

As discussed in chapter 3, the social organization of stores contributes to this gender hierarchy. The demand for employee "flexibility" effectively prevents those with other obligations from gaining a foothold in retail at the lower levels and from achieving management positions higher up. Because many stores are now open "round the clock," managers increasingly rely on part-time workers to fill in as needed (Robinson 1995). This practice disadvantages workers who require regular schedules to combine with their child care and other domestic responsibilities—still considered women's work in our society. For this reason, guaranteed, stable hours are crucial for attracting, retaining, and promoting women workers.

Relegating men and women, whites and minorities, to different sales tasks also promotes inequality. As I argued in chapter 3, this practice is based on stereotypes and perpetuates stereotypes. Although ultimately managers decide on the division of tasks within stores, the issue is complicated because workers sort themselves (and each other) into positions based on race and gender. I saw this when Deshay resisted register duty, when Robert performed a drag routine in the Barbie department, and when my co-workers mocked the only women in the storerooms. Granted, I think that men do this more than women, but occupational segregation reflects (and reproduces) general cultural norms shared by many, if not most, members of our society. This makes challenges to it especially tricky. Personally, I preferred selling Barbies to selling Game Boys, and I'm still not convinced that this is wrong or bad. I think that gender segregation is problematic only when tasks preferred by women and nonwhite men are remunerated less or evaluated less favorably when promotion time rolls around. In principle, I agree that an ideal society would be one where equal numbers of men and women worked in every job, but in practice, I'm willing to live in a gender-segregated social world as long as it is monitored to ensure equal pay for jobs of comparable worth.

The question of what to buy is equally fraught. Toys reflect and bolster gender and race stereotypes too. As I argued in chapter 4, many adults seek out toys that represent the race and gender identity they wish for the child recipient, and children are all too eager to embrace the hegemonic masculinity and emphasized femininity of popular toys. The few adults who object to gendered toys no doubt face disappointed children who scowl at the alternatives they offer, like the grandmother who insisted on buying "Get Real Girl" for her granddaughter. Personally, I think it is good (and fun) to make "gender trouble" in the selection of toys. When Mike Messner (2000) bought a Barbie for his ten-year-old son, I applauded his effort to challenge the conventional socialization of boys. But as public policy, buying Barbies for boys is not a solution to gender inequality. Because items in material culture have a vast array of meanings (Best 1998; Lord 1994), adults can never be sure of the impact of their choices on children. Encouraging subversion and criticism seems like a better approach to challenging gender and racial stereotypes than buying only politically correct toys. Perhaps that is what play is all about.

SHOPPING VALUES VERSUS VALUE SHOPPING

I come from a family of bargain hunters who consider paying full price a lapse of moral and intellectual judgment. In my family, the joy of purchasing a deeply discounted item can (and often does) outweigh the pleasures of ownership. We sometimes leave the price tags on gifts as evidence of the bargain price we paid, a celebration of the shared family commitment to value shopping.

Everybody loves a bargain. As Daniel Miller (1998) wittily observes, most people shop to save money and save money to shop. This paradox underlies the success of the large discount chains like Wal-Mart and Target, which advertise "low prices" before mentioning the desirable features of the items they sell. These discount stores are immensely successful: their massive purchasing power, used to undercut their competition's pricing, is putting specialty stores like the Toy Warehouse and Diamond Toys at risk for going out of business.

This cultural practice of "saving through shopping" has a hand in reproducing the social and economic inequalities I have described in this book. To transform the social conditions of shopping, consumers must become skeptical about prices that are very low. Shoppers must learn to ask, "Who is subsidizing this price?" Usually low prices are subsidized by the workers who make the products (especially overseas) and by service workers who earn below living wages (Ehrenreich 2001).[5]

This isn't to say we should all shop at expensive boutiques. The consumer citizen also should be skeptical about high-end shopping. When seeking exclusivity and high status, consumers need to ask, "Who is left out (of the store and of the purchase)? Who am I distinguishing myself from?" (Schor 1998). Do higher prices translate into better working conditions for labor? Or higher profits for huge corporations?

Unfortunately, individual consumers have no way of knowing the answers to these questions because all we see on product labels are the price, the contents, and the country of origin. As James Farrell (2003) argues, price tags tell us how cheaply a manufacturer can produce that toy, not the full cost of the item. That would require figuring in the economic value, social and environmental costs, ethical and spiritual costs, and opportunity costs of production. He writes, "We need to remember that the lowest price isn't always the best price. In fact, the lowest price can often indicate the highest long-term cost" (283).

During the Progressive Era, a number of popular campaigns sought to educate the public about the social and economic conditions of production. When *Consumer Reports* debuted, information about factory conditions was included in the description and assessment of goods. (According to Cohen [2003], this practice was stopped when the organization came under suspicion of communist infiltration during the Cold War.) In my view, consumer labels on the products we buy should contain information on worker wages. "Fair trade" coffee is an example of this effort that could be expanded to other commodities. I suggest taking this a step further by labeling products to certify fair labor standards not only for the workers who make the goods but also for the clerks who sell them.[6]

Union label campaigns have existed for over a hundred years. But according to Lawrence Glickman (1997), the early union label movement foundered on the shoals of gender politics. Men who were union members felt uncomfortable relying on their consuming wives to look for the union label; apparently this threatened their masculinity and the masculinity of working-class politics. An even more critical blow to the union label movement was its contradiction with the working-class ideal of thrift. A storekeeper complained to a sociologist writing in 1903 that workers "want to receive union wages, but don't want to pay union prices" (127). Although union labels can educate the public about the conditions of production, they offer no immediate benefit to the individual consumer, making the strategy more idealistic than practical. Thus, in the fight against sweated labor, enforcement of labor laws is ultimately a better approach than labeling. But labeling may be one means to raise awareness that can then provoke the public to demand a renewed commitment to higher labor standards and better enforcement of labor law.

Few products today carry the union label, but most are now labeled with the country of origin. Many consumers seek out products made in America because they want to keep manufacturing jobs in this country or because they think that if a product is made in the United States the workers who made it were paid fair wages and treated humanely. Thus they think that "made in America" means "made by workers earning fair wages in decent conditions." But labels can be misleading. In this day of sophisticated advertising, when every product promises to enhance our health, environment, and social values, it should come as no surprise that "made in America" does not mean that the workers who made the products were treated well.

In an eye-opening book on the "Buy American" campaigns of the twentieth century, Dana Frank (1999) observes that racism and xenophobia often lie beneath efforts to promote American-made products to American consumers.[7] The "Crafted with Pride in the USA" label, for example, was spearheaded by conservative businessmen Sam Walton (of Wal-Mart) and Roger Milliken (whose fortune from textiles supported the 1992 presidential campaign of Patrick Buchanan).

Starting in the 1980s, Walton promised to buy American. His goal was to attract patriotic Americans to his stores. Giant banners were displayed over goods purportedly made in America.

Television exposés in the 1990s found that some of the so-called made in America goods were actually made by child laborers in Bangladesh (Frank 1999, 201). But even many of the goods that were, in fact, made in America were manufactured in sweatshops. Factory conditions deteriorated in this country in part because of the growth of giant retailers, as described in chapter 2. By the late 1980s, retailers like Wal-Mart had unprecedented power over manufacturers and suppliers. Because Wal-Mart controlled a large share of the mass market, it could demand certain prices from suppliers who were increasingly dependent on it to stock their goods. Wal-Mart could insist that its suppliers locate their factories in America, but it could also demand the lowest price from them, and if that wasn't supplied, it would just leave, forcing the supplier into bankruptcy (202). Frank concludes that Wal-Mart and the other low-cost retailers "foster precarious manufacturing jobs [in the United States] in which suppliers are forced to drive down their labor costs and prices to satisfy an ever voracious and fickle buyer. Unions have no place in Wal-Mart's America" (207). According to Frank, Sam Walton himself acknowledged that "Wal-Mart was only buying American if the products available were of the same price and quality as comparable imports" (205).

Protecting American manufacturing jobs against foreign competition ignores the fact of globalization and pits workers against each other on the basis of race and nation. Instead, I agree with Frank that consumers should be concerned about the economic and social conditions of all workers, not only those in their country. Protecting workers' jobs in this country will not prevent exploitation. If these are bad American jobs, lacking benefits and living wages, they are not worth protecting. If these are good

American jobs, companies will flee to countries where they can turn them into bad jobs. As long as they are allowed to do it, corporations will seek the lowest price for labor. An international alliance of workers is needed to halt the relentless march of capitalism to the bottom. Racism and xenophobia prevent this alliance, playing into the economic interests of retailers who are always on the lookout for the cheapest labor.

CONCLUSION

The model of consumer citizenship advocated by Cohen would transform the toy-shopping experience. Instead of being guided by the lowest price or social status, consumers would pay attention to the working conditions of the employees who manufacture and sell the merchandise. Citizen consumers would also pay attention to the race and gender diversity in where they shop, how they shop, and what they buy. Government has a central role to play in bringing about these transformations, but only through consumer-worker alliances will government be forced to confront and to constrain capital.

Hopefully, as the service sector increases in size, consumer-worker alliances will grow. But as they are currently constituted, the social conditions of the retail industry reflect consumers' fundamental disregard for retail workers. In my experience, toy store shoppers rarely demonstrate respect for retail workers. Consumers must learn to see themselves in the shoes of those who serve them. Children will learn to treat service workers respectfully when they see their parents doing the same.

Many books on consumerism end with a plea for the transformation of cultural values, and in some ways this book is no different. A renewed commitment to the values of the citizen consumer is necessary to bring about changes in the retail industry. Justice, equality, and democracy should be compatible with shopping, not left behind in the parking lot. But as I have emphasized in this chapter, new values alone cannot alter the social relations of consumption. The political economy of shopping must also change. The retail industry must be reined in by new legislation mandating worker rights to living wages, health care, and equal opportunities. Citizen consumers hold the key to this challenge.

NOTES

CHAPTER I. A SOCIOLOGIST INSIDE TOY STORES

1. "Toy Warehouse," "Diamond Toys," and the names of the workers are all pseudonyms.

2. There are a number of exceptions, several of whom I discuss in this chapter.

3. MacLean was a member of the Chicago Women's School of Sociology, a group of women researchers inspired by the works of Jane Addams who used their scholarship to promote progressive social change. A Canadian immigrant, MacLean came to the United States to study at the University of Chicago and became the first woman to receive a master's degree in sociology and the second to receive a Ph.D. Her contributions to American sociology are discussed in Lengermann and Niebrugge-Brantley (1998).

Sociologists were involved in significant ways in the study and analysis of consumerism at two other times in American history. During the 1930s and 1940s, W. E. B. Du Bois and Robert Lynd were leaders in (separate) struggles for consumers' rights and their access to stores and shopping. Later, in the 1950s, sociologists teamed up with marketing professionals to apply their insights on group behavior to consumers, forming the famed Survey Research Center at the University of Michigan, which paved the way to targeted advertising and market segmentation. See Cohen (2003).

4. I should have known about this study. MacLean was an important sociologist in her day. One reason I didn't is the legacy of sexism in the history of the discipline. In the 1920s, the men of the Chicago school took deliberate steps to distance themselves and what they considered the science of sociology from the progressive work of Jane Addams (upon whose work the school was founded) and the members of the Chicago Women's School of Sociology. See Deegan (1988).

5. I also chose to study toy stores because I wrongly assumed they

were businesses that hired only women. In the past I've studied men and women in nontraditional or gender-atypical occupations (for example, women in the military, men in nursing), and I wanted to focus instead on women who work in predominantly female jobs to understand gender segregation from their points of view. But as I discovered, a large number of men work in these stores, though most are either in the back rooms assembling the toys or in the front rooms managing the employees.

6. As I write from my home in Austin, Texas, in 2003, Wal-Mart is fighting local city ordinances that limit construction on top of the city's environmentally sensitive aquifer, which supplies drinking water and recreational facilities to the population. Wal-Mart is planning to build three giant supercenters within fifteen miles of each other; according to a spokesperson, their ultimate goal is build one Wal-Mart every three miles (Smith 2003, 23). To date, public protest and city council efforts have resulted in delays but have not stopped Wal-Mart's development plans.

7. As I will discuss in the next chapter, the big box Toy Warehouse is facing intense competition from the "even bigger box" Wal-Mart chain of stores. Wal-Mart is currently the largest seller of toys in the United States and, probably, the world (Michman and Mazze 2001).

CHAPTER 2. HISTORY OF TOY SHOPPING IN AMERICA

1. Among the towns and cities where I lived were Chandler, Arizona; Sherman, Texas; Selma, Alabama; Fort Walton Beach, Florida; and Enid, Oklahoma. Other members of air force families in the 1960s and 1970s will surely identify the connection between these places.

2. Researchers disagree about whether manufacturers or retailers today have the upper hand in their relationship. Brand loyalty is still very strong among consumers, giving manufacturers some power in their dealings with stores. Farris and Ailawadi (1992) review a number of reasons why structural changes in the manufacturer-retailer relationship have not always resulted in greater power (and profits) for grocery store retailers.

3. Another famous discounter at the turn of the century was Filene's department store. "Filene's Basement" became a spectacular success for offering deep discounts on the same goods that had been available earlier in the season in the upstairs levels of the store. But once fair trade policies were instituted, discounters were limited to offering products with unfamiliar labels and of unknown quality. See Bluestone et al. (1981).

4. Diamond Toys is not a discounter, so it is not technically a category killer. Instead of offering low prices, Diamond Toys uses a marketing strategy of luring customers by promising expert advice and a range of services. This recalls the strategies of the original department stores, which appealed to the pretensions of the middle-class shopper aspiring to upper-class status by offering a range of luxury services, including home delivery, shopping advice and assistance, and elaborate and elegant store fixtures.

5. A. T. Stewart, the largest New York City department store in the 1800s, hired only men as sales attendants for the same reason that Macy's excluded them. According to Hower (1943, 193), Stewart "hired the handsomest men he could obtain as clerks because he noticed that ladies who shopped in his store like to gossip and even to flirt with them. Stewart's nice young men were so popular that other stores used the same tactics."

6. The retail industry as a whole experienced a conversion from full-time to part-time staffing in the 1970s and 1980s, a period that corresponds with a surge of employment in this sector. Retail jobs increased by 68 percent between 1973 and 1993, compared to an overall job growth of 43 percent (Tilly 1996, 25). According to Tilly, most of that growth was in part-time jobs. Employers in retail establishments prefer to hire part-time workers because they are paid less, receive fewer benefits, can work extra shifts or hours without accruing overtime pay, and have the reputation of being harder to unionize. Although many workers prefer part-time to full-time schedules, involuntary part-time employment increased steadily between 1969 and 1993 at a rate of 0.12 percentage points per year (164).

7. I am indebted to Robert Zussman for his insights into this matter. He draws a felicitous comparison between retail clerks and restaurant workers, noting that high-priced, fancy restaurants prefer to hire white middle-class men (and women, who are often required to dress like men—in tuxedos, for example) to symbolize their refinement, while fast-food restaurants are less pretentious and thus more diverse in their labor practices. Part of what is being sold in a fancy restaurant is the solicitous attention of a professional wait staff. Professionalism is equated with white masculinity, so white men are the preferred hires. In down-market restaurants, in contrast, interaction with the wait staff is minimized and often highly routinized. Consequently, it matters less to the restaurant's image what people are hired to staff the counter (as long as they smile and are cheerful), so fast-food workers are more racially diverse. Cobble's (1991) history of waitressing makes a similar argument. She describes how race, gender, and social class determined the hiring practices at restaurants in the early twentieth century. However, in contrast to retail work, black men were often hired to serve in upscale restaurants, which she interprets as a legacy of slavery.

8. As I will discuss later in the book, social class shapes parents' approaches to child rearing. According to Annette Lareau (2003), middle-class parents typically treat children's leisure as an opportunity to cultivate and refine their tastes and skills, whereas working-class parents seem to prefer to let children choose their own entertainment apart from adult supervision. This is reflected in media consumption. For example, Seiter (1993) claims that middle-class parents have a stronger antipathy toward children's watching TV than do working-class parents. Sternheimer (2003) believes this difference is because working-class and poor parents have a better grasp than middle-class parents of the true sources of harm to children. She writes, "Lower income people have more experience with the reality of problems like violence to know that the media are not a big part of the equation in their struggles to keep their children safe in troubled communities" (40).

CHAPTER 3. THE SOCIAL ORGANIZATION OF TOY STORES

1. This is not the "ideal worker" sought by employers at the fast-food restaurants in Harlem studied by Katherine Newman (1999). She found that young people under twenty-two were disproportionately rejected for job openings in the mid-1990s. More than half of new hires were older than twenty-three. Nevertheless, the retail and fast-food industries continue to justify their low wages and meager benefits on the basis of this "ideal worker" who doesn't "need" their job to support himself or herself economically. This is how Wal-Mart justifies its minimal payment of employee health care benefits. After a series of news reports lambasting the store for its failure to provide health care coverage for most workers, a Wal-Mart spokesperson maintained that most of those who are not covered by Wal-Mart benefits are "senior citizens on Medicare, students covered by their parents' policies, or employees with second jobs or working spouses" (Abelson 2004, A13). This is the historic argument for not paying living wages to women—they don't really "need" the money from their work because they are members of families with access to a male wage (see Kessler-Harris 1990). This argument justifies unequal pay for equal work (which is illegal under Title VII) and undermines all workers' rights to fair compensation.

2. Men make more money than women in most occupations. Among sales workers employed in the general category "retail and personal services," men earn on average $488 per week, and women earn $326, a ratio of .67. (These numbers are the 2002 median weekly earnings of full-time workers.) If we take out workers employed in some of the most gender-segregated stores (those selling motor vehicles, apparel, furniture, appliances, hardware, and parts), men earn on average $466 per week, and women earn $353, a ratio of .76. (This reflects the income of workers in the category "Sales workers, other commodities.") This information is from U.S. Bureau of Labor Statistics (2002).

3. The National Association for the Advancement of Colored People (NAACP) issued a report in 2003 claiming that the retail trade industry, compared to other industries, is especially notorious for discriminating

against African Americans. This report, which ranked forty-five large retail companies on employment opportunities, marketing procurement, community reinvestment, and charitable donations, gave the industry a "D" average (compared to "C" for the lodging, telecommunications, and banking industries).

4. See Burawoy (1980), Freeman (2000), Hossfeld (1990), Milkman (1997), and Salzinger (2000).

5. Notable exceptions include Hochschild (1983), Leidner (1993), Glazer (1993), and Talwar (2002). I speculate that the production focus of most sociology is due to the association of retail work with consumption, long considered women's work, instead of production, which is generally considered a higher-status male domain. Lizabeth Cohen (2003) argues that this split is a legacy of the Progressive Era, when the two issues were uncoupled politically, with women spearheading movements for consumer rights and men spearheading movements for worker rights.

6. Although I was hired to be a cashier, my actual job involved many other tasks. When there were no customers ready to check out, I was on the floor helping customers find things, giving them advice, straightening shelves, returning merchandise to its proper location, and so on. My job involved constant interacting, chatting, joking, complaining, and goofing off with other staff members, not only while we were doing our jobs, but also while we were on break and while we were straightening the store after closing.

7. Robert Zussman's careful reading of this text inspired this insight, for which I am grateful.

8. The Toy Warehouse also cut labor costs by not supplying benefits to most employees. The store claimed to offer subsidized health insurance and paid vacations to its workers, and indeed some of the full-time workers told me that they received these benefits. But most of us worked part time and didn't receive any benefits. During orientation, we were shown a video that described these employee benefits. According to the video, we had to sign up for benefits during our first thirty days of employment, but we wouldn't be eligible until we had passed our three-month probation period. The video assured us that our manager would

let us know when we were eligible. When I asked Olive how to sign up, she deferred my question, and I decided not to push it. I later learned that part-time workers had to work at least twenty hours per week for three months to be eligible for the benefits program, which is probably another reason why our hours kept getting cut.

9. Talwar (2002) observes that in the fast-food industry firing is rarely a direct action. Instead, managers typically reduce hours or schedule workers for undesirable hours (very early or very late). She writes, "Such employees are eventually forced to quit on their own, and the employer escapes having to pay unemployment insurance" (58). My sense is that this is what was occurring at the Toy Warehouse. Employees would quit in often dramatic, highly principled, public scenes, which were gratifying and cathartic but ultimately played into the interests of management.

10. According to the National Retail Federation, the employee turnover rate is between 100 percent and 160 percent for part-time workers and 80 percent to 120 percent for full-time workers (cited in Steen 2003). Data published by the U.S. Bureau of Labor Statistics (2005) show that the monthly turnover rate in retail is about 5 to 6 percent, or 60 to 72 percent per year, one of the highest rates in any industry.

11. The rules governing breaks and lunch periods are established by the state's labor laws. In the state where I worked, those who work four hours are guaranteed a paid fifteen-minute break. Those scheduled for longer than 6.5 hours are required to take a thirty-minute lunch break off the clock. Those scheduled for longer than 7.5 hours are entitled to a second paid fifteen-minute break. Workers younger than eighteen are required by law to take longer breaks. At the Toy Warehouse, I was often scheduled for seven-hour shifts but then required to stay an extra hour or more at closing, which meant that I wasn't scheduled for the second break.

CHAPTER 4. INEQUALITY ON THE SHOPPING FLOOR

1. Diane Ehrensaft (1997) finds that middle-class parents typically buy "older" toys for their children to encourage accelerated development.

2. See Majors and Billson (1992) for a discussion of this dynamic.

3. See Ferguson (2000) for a discussion of these racialized and gendered interpretations of insubordination in schools.

4. I thank Dana Britton for her comments and insights into this matter.

5. This discussion of control was inspired by numerous conversations with Allison Pugh, who writes on children and consumption.

CHAPTER 5. KIDS IN TOYLAND

1. Bourdieu's major relevant work on this topic is *Distinction* (1984). My discussion also relies on David Swartz's excellent introduction, *Culture and Power: The Sociology of Pierre Bourdieu* (1997) and Bourdieu and Wacquant (1992).

2. According to Viviana Zelizer (1985), this shift in emphasis from saving to spending occurred even earlier in the child-rearing advice literature. In the 1930s, experts urged parents to give children a regular allowance in order to train them to be efficient shoppers. The rise of a consumer society, she shows, demanded a child "who spends wisely, saves wisely and gives wisely" (106).

3. It is important to distinguish my use of the term *sadomasochism* from other definitions and usages. In the clinically based psychoanalytic literature, *sadomasochism* refers to a complex character disposition in which an individual gains sexual pleasure from punishing or by being punished by others; sometimes this condition is treated as a psychological pathology. Another use of the term is to describe theatrical playacting involving props such as whips and chains and leather clothing. Individuals who enjoy this play or incorporate these elements in their dress may or may not be driven by underlying sadomasochistic character dispositions. In contrast, I am using the term to refer to a specific relationship dynamic that does not necessarily involve either the character traits labeled "pathological" by clinicians or the mutually respectful sex play defended by some feminists. Following Chancer (1993, 1998) and Benjamin (1988), I am using the term to describe an intimate relationship in

which one individual assumes a dominant and controlling position and the other willingly submits to his or her subordination. I draw on a similar analysis to understand specific cases of institutionalized sexual harassment in Williams (2002).

4. Some of my coworkers commented to me that they would never bring their children into the store for this reason. For instance, noting the high number of screaming children, Chauntelle told me that bringing a child into the Toy Warehouse was a form of child torture. Poor and working-class parents had limited economic resources to spend on toys. To shield their children from inevitable disappointment, some thought it best to keep them out of the toy store.

5. There may be a class difference in adults' use of toys to reward children for good behavior. Allison Pugh (2004) found that in poor and working-class families, money is not predictably available to reward children for completing homework or doing chores. When parents do purchase gifts, the links to behavior are not immediate and consequently send the message "I appreciate you" instead of "I appreciate what you did" (242). Ironically, Pugh notes, this approach is praised in middle-class child-rearing texts, yet it is not the message that these poor and working-class adults necessary want to communicate to their children. From their kids' perspectives, she argues, money (and gifts) "became something you got when you were lucky, not because you were good" (244).

6. I am not arguing that money and gifts are incompatible with meaningful, loving relationships. Following Viviana Zelizer (2004), I reject the view that money and love represent "hostile worlds." The hostile worlds perspective is the belief that "the entry of instrumental means such as monetization and cost accounting into the worlds of caring, friendship, sexuality, parent-child relations, and personal information depletes them of their richness, hence that zones of intimacy thrive only if people erect effective barriers around them" (124). Instead, I agree with Zelizer that money and gifts have negotiated meanings that emerge in interactions. However, I do believe that consumer culture encourages us to equate "buying something" with "loving someone," privileging economic exchange as the principal and best means of expressing affection.

7. Similarly, Arlie Hochschild (2004, 50) argues that consumerism promises to resolve adults' psychological ambivalence around care. She observes that when we "buy goods and services that promise a family-like experience . . . we also pursue the fantasy of a life free from ambivalence." Likewise, she maintains that "commercial substitutes for family life do not eliminate ambivalence" but merely express our contradictory yearnings for intimacy and autonomy.

CHAPTER 6. TOYS AND CITIZENSHIP

1. Pierrette Hondagneu-Sotelo (2001) discusses various forms of domestic service. The "au pair" is a live-in domestic worker who is a young, white woman from either Europe or rural America. The au pair is contrasted with the live-in domestic who is an immigrant from the third world. Typically, au pairs are paid more money, their duties are more limited, and they have more autonomy than third-world women domestics.

2. The demand for a living wage is not new. It was first endorsed by labor leaders in the late nineteenth century, but it fell out of favor from the 1930s to the 1980s. See Glickman (1997).

3. The television exposé was on Bill Moyers's *NOW,* aired on public broadcasting stations in summer 2003. A study by the Center for Labor Research and Education at the University of California, Berkeley, finds that, in California, nearly half of public assistance money goes to families with at least one member in the labor force. This is a form of public subsidy for low-wage employers. Retail and food service were cited as the worst offenders in this regard: working families in retail and food service collected about $2 billion in public assistance, far exceeding workers in sectors such as manufacturing, construction, hospitality, or agriculture. See Zabin, Dube, and Jacobs (2004).

4. Dan Clawson (2003) is concerned that living-wage campaigns may be disempowering to workers. Insofar as these organizing efforts take place on behalf of workers but do not include workers, he fears that they may promote dependency and passivity of labor.

5. In New York City, a group of consumers in Greenwich Village has

organized to urge local stores to raise the wages of retail workers. This group, made up of several churches, community groups, and labor unions in the area, is also urging stores to provide health care benefits and opportunities for unionizing among their employees. The director of the project called it an attempt to build an "economic justice zone." Predictably, store owners are worried that higher wages and benefits will result in higher prices for consumers, leading them to shop elsewhere. See Greenhouse (2004, A18).

6. Another idea, suggested to me by Allison Pugh, is to distribute cards or fliers to consumers with a list of names of "fair trade" toy manufacturers and retailers. This follows the model of the Monterey Bay Aquarium, which distributes cards to its patrons listing the fish that are ecologically sound to buy and consume.

7. Similarly, the union label movement had its start in an 1874 xenophobic campaign against Chinese labor (Glickman 1997, 108).

REFERENCES

Abelson, Reed. 2004. "States Are Battling against Wal-Mart over Health Care." *New York Times,* November 1, A1, A13.

Acker, Joan. 1990. "Hierarchies, Jobs, Bodies: A Theory of Gendered Organizations." *Gender & Society* 4: 139–58.

Adamson, Jim. 2000. *The Denny's Story: How a Company in Crisis Resurrected Its Good Name and Reputation.* New York: John Wiley.

Amirault, Thomas. 1997. "Characteristics of Multiple Jobholders, 1995." *Monthly Labor Review* 120 (March): 9–15.

Andrews, Cecile. 2000. "Simplicity Circles and the Compulsive Shopper." In *I Shop Therefore I Am: Compulsive Buying and the Search for Self,* ed. April Lane Benson, 484–96. Northvale, NJ: Jason Aronson.

Aslaksen, Iulie. 2002. "Gender Constructions and the Possibility of a Generous Economic Actor." *Hypatia* 17 (Spring): 118–32.

Benjamin, Jessica. 1988. *The Bonds of Love: Psychoanalysis, Feminism and the Problem of Domination.* New York: Pantheon.

Benson, Susan Porter. 1986. *Counter Cultures: Saleswomen, Managers, and Customers in American Department Stores, 1890–1940.* Urbana: University of Illinois Press.

Best, Joel. 1998. "Too Much Fun: Toys as Social Problems and the Interpretation of Culture." *Symbolic Interaction* 21(2): 197–212.

Bluestone, Barry, Patricia Hanna, Sarah Kuhn, and Laura Moore. 1981. *The Retail Revolution: Market Transformation, Investment, and Labor in the Modern Department Store.* Boston: Auburn House.

Blumer, Herbert. 1969. *Symbolic Interactionism.* Berkeley: University of California Press.

Bourdieu, Pierre. 1984. *Distinction: A Social Critique of the Judgement of Taste.* Cambridge, MA: Harvard University Press.

Bourdieu, Pierre, and Löic Wacquant. 1992. *An Invitation to Reflexive Sociology.* Chicago: University of Chicago Press.

Brecher, Edward M. 1949a. "Buying at a Discount: Is It against the Law?" *Consumer Reports* 14 (September): 420–23.

————. 1949b. "Discount Houses." *Consumer Reports* 14 (August): 343–45, 375.

Burawoy, Michael. 1980. *Manufacturing Consent*. Chicago: University of Chicago Press.

Butler, Dan. 2004. "Perspectives from the Board Room." Paper presented at the Consumer Racial Profiling Conference, University of Texas, Austin, March 30.

Center for a New American Dream. 2003. "Facts about Marketing to Children." Retrieved May 29, 2003, from www.newdream.org/kids/facts.php.

Chancer, Lynn S. 1992. *Sadomasochism in Everyday Life: The Dynamics of Power and Powerlessness*. New Brunswick, NJ: Rutgers University Press.

————. 1998. *Reconcilable Differences: Confronting Beauty, Pornography, and the Future of Feminism*. Berkeley: University of California Press.

Cheever, Ben. 2001. *Selling Ben Cheever: Back to Square One in a Service Economy*. New York: Bloomsbury.

Chin, Elizabeth. 2001. *Purchasing Power: Black Kids and American Consumer Culture*. Minneapolis: University of Minnesota Press.

Clawson, Dan. 2003. *The Next Upsurge: Labor and the New Social Movements*. Ithaca, NY: ILR Press.

Cobble, Dorothy Sue. 1991. *Dishing It Out: Waitresses and Their Unions in the Twentieth Century*. Urbana: University of Illinois Press.

Cohen, Lizabeth. 1998. "From Town Center to Shopping Center: The Reconfiguration of Community Marketplaces in Postwar America." In *His and Hers: Gender, Consumption, and Technology*, ed. Roger Horowitz and Arwen Mohun, 189–234. Charlottesville: University Press of Virginia.

————. 2003. *A Consumers' Republic: The Politics of Mass Consumption in Postwar America*. New York: Knopf.

Collins, Patricia Hill. 2000. *Black Feminist Thought*. New York: Routledge.

Connell, R. W. 1995. *Masculinities*. Berkeley: University of California Press.

Cook, Daniel Thomas. 2000. "The Other Child Study: Figuring Children as Consumers in Market Research, 1910s–1990s." *Sociological Quarterly* 41(3): 487–507.

Corstjens, Judith, and Marcel Corstjens. 1995. *Store Wars: The Battle for Mindspace and Shelfspace*. Chichester: John Wiley.

Deegan, Mary Jo. 1988. *Jane Addams and the Men of the Chicago School, 1892–1918*. New Brunswick, NJ: Transaction.

Ehrenreich, Barbara. 2001. *Nickel and Dimed: On (Not) Getting By in America*. New York: Metropolitan Books.

Ehrensaft, Diane. 1997. *Spoiling Childhood: How Well-Meaning Parents Are Giving Children Too Much—But Not What They Need*. New York: Guilford.

Emerson, Rana. 2002. "Where My Girls At? Negotiating Black Womanhood in Music Videos." *Gender & Society* 16: 115–35.

Farrell, James. 2003. *One Nation under Goods: Malls and the Seductions of American Shopping*. Washington, DC: Smithsonian Books.

Farris, Paul W., and Kusum L. Ailawadi. 1992. "Retail Power: Monster or Mouse?" *Journal of Retailing* 68(4): 351–69.

Feagin, Joe, and Melvin Sikes. 1995. *Living with Racism: The Black Middle Class Experience*. New York: Beacon.

Ferguson, Ann Arnet. 2000. *Bad Boys: Public Schools in the Making of Black Masculinity*. Ann Arbor: University of Michigan Press.

Folbre, Nancy. 2001. *The Invisible Heart: Economics and Family Values*. New York: New Press.

Frank, Dana. 1999. *Buy American: The Untold Story of Economic Nationalism*. Boston: Beacon Press.

Freeman, Carla. 2000. *High Tech and High Heels in the Global Economy: Women, Work, and Pink Collar Identities in the Caribbean*. Durham, NC: Duke University Press.

Gabriel, Yiannis. 2004. "The Glass Cage: Flexible Work, Fragmented Consumption, Fragile Selves." In *Self, Social Structure, and Beliefs*, ed. Jeffrey Alexander, Gary Marx, and Christine Williams, 57–73. Berkeley: University of California Press.

Gerstenberg, Karl, and T. Dart Ellsworth. 1949. "Who Wears the Pants in Department and Specialty Stores? A Survey of Women Executives in Retailing." *Journal of Retailing* 25 (Fall): 97–123.

Gherardi, Sylvia. 1995. *Gender, Symbolism and Organizational Culture.* Thousand Oaks, CA: Sage Publications.

Glazer, Nona. 1993. *Women's Paid and Unpaid Labor: The Work Transfer in Health Care and Retailing.* Philadelphia: Temple University Press.

Glickman, Lawrence B. 1997. *A Living Wage: American Workers and the Making of Consumer Society.* Ithaca, NY: Cornell University Press.

Goffman, Erving. 1967. *Interaction Ritual: Essays on Face to Face Behavior.* Garden City, NY: Anchor Books.

———. 1977. "The Arrangement between the Sexes." *Theory and Society* 4: 301–31.

Greenhouse, Steven. 2002. "Suits Say Wal-Mart Forces Workers to Toil off the Clock." *New York Times,* June 25, A1, A20.

———. 2003. "Abercrombie & Fitch Accused of Discrimination in Hiring." *New York Times,* June 17, A1.

———. 2004. "Customers Take up the Cause of Higher Pay at Some Stores." *New York Times,* October 18, A18.

Hanchett, Thomas W. 1996. "U.S. Tax Policy and the Shopping-Center Boom of the 1950s and 1960s." *American Historical Review* 101 (October): 1082–1110.

Harris, Anne-Marie G. 2003. "Shopping while Black: Applying 42 U.S.C. § 1981 to Cases of Consumer Racial Profiling." *Boston College Third World Law Journal* 23: 1–56.

Hebdige, Dick. 1979. *Subculture: The Meaning of Style.* London: Methuen.

Hendershot, Heather. 1998. *Saturday Morning Censors: Television Regulation before the V-Chip.* Durham, NC: Duke University Press.

Henderson, Geraldine. 2004. "Perspectives from the Classroom." Paper presented at the Consumer Racial Profiling Conference, University of Texas, Austin, March 30.

Hine, Thomas. 2002. *I Want That! How We All Became Shoppers.* New York: HarperCollins.

Hochschild, Arlie. 1983. *The Managed Heart: Commercialization of Human Feeling.* Berkeley: University of California Press.

———. 1997. *The Time Bind: When Work Becomes Home and Home Becomes Work.* New York: Metropolitan Books.

———. 2004. "The Commodity Frontier." In *Self, Social Structure, and Beliefs,* ed. Jeffrey Alexander, Gary Marx, and Christine Williams, 38–56. Berkeley: University of California Press.

Hollander, Stanley. 1986 [1954]. *Discount Retailing.* New York: Garland Publishing.

Hondagneu-Sotelo, Pierrette. 2001. *Doméstica: Immigrant Workers Cleaning and Caring in the Shadows of Affluence.* Berkeley: University of California Press.

Hossfeld, Karen. 1990. "Their Logic against Them: Contradictions in Sex, Race, and Class in Silicon Valley." In *Women Workers and Global Restructuring,* ed. Kathryn Ward, 149–78. Ithaca, NY: ILR Press.

Hower, Ralph M. 1943. *History of Macy's of New York, 1858–1919.* Cambridge, MA: Harvard University Press.

Humphery, Kim. 1998. *Shelf Life: Supermarkets and the Changing Cultures of Consumption.* Cambridge: Cambridge University Press.

Kellner, Douglas. 1999. "Theorizing/Resisting McDonaldization: A Multiperspectivist Approach." In *Resisting McDonaldization,* ed. Barry Smart, 186–206. Thousand Oaks, CA: Sage Publications.

Kessler-Harris, Ann. 1990. *A Woman's Wage.* Lexington: University of Kentucky Press.

Kline, Stephen. 1993. *Out of the Garden: Toys, TV, and Children's Culture in the Age of Marketing.* New York: Verso.

Lareau, Annette. 2003. *Unequal Childhoods: Class, Race, and Family Life.* Berkeley: University of California Press.

Leidner, Robin. 1993. *Fast Food, Fast Talk: Service Work and the Routinization of Everyday Life.* Berkeley: University of California Press.

Lengermann, Patricia Madoo, and Jill Niebrugge-Brantley. 1998. *The Women Founders: Sociology and Social Theory, 1830–1930.* Boston: McGraw Hill.

Levy, Frank. 1998. *The New Dollars and Dreams: American Incomes and Economic Change.* New York: Russell Sage Foundation.

Lichtenstein, Nelson. 2002. *State of the Union: A Century of American Labor.* Princeton, NJ: Princeton University Press.

Linn, Susan. 2004. *Consuming Kids: The Hostile Takeover of Childhood.* New York: New Press.

Loe, Meika. 1996. "Working for Men: At the Intersection of Power, Gender, and Sexuality." *Sociological Inquiry* 66: 399–421.

Lord, M. G. 1994. *Forever Barbie.* New York: Morrow.

MacLean, Annie Marion. 1899. "Two Weeks in Department Stores." *American Journal of Sociology* 4 (May): 721–41.

Majors, Richard, and Janet Mancini Billson. 1992. *Cool Pose: The Dilemmas of Black Manhood in America.* New York: Simon and Schuster.

Martin, Christopher R. 2004. *Framed! Labor and the Corporate Media.* Ithaca, NY: Cornell University Press.

Marx, Karl. 1978 [1867]. *Capital.* Vol. 1. Excerpted in *The Marx-Engels Reader,* 2d ed., ed. Robert C. Tucker. New York: Norton.

Mayer, Robert N. 1989. *The Consumer Movement: Guardians of the Marketplace.* Boston: Twayne Publishers.

McCall, Leslie. 2001. *Complex Inequality: Gender, Class and Race in the New Economy.* New York: Routledge.

McDonough, Yona Zeldis, ed. 1999. *The Barbie Chronicles.* New York: Touchstone.

McNeal, James. 1999. *The Kids' Market: Myths and Realities.* Ithaca, NY: Paramount Market Publishing.

McRobbie, Angela. 1991. *Feminism and Youth Culture.* Boston: Unwin Hyman.

Messner, Michael. 2000. "Barbie Girls versus Sea Monsters: Children Constructing Gender." *Gender & Society* 14(6): 765–84.

Michman, Ronald D., and Edward M. Mazze. 2001. *Specialty Retailers: Marketing Triumphs and Blunders.* Westport, CT: Quorum Books.

Milkman, Ruth. 1997. *Farewell to the Factory: Auto Workers in the Late Twentieth Century.* Berkeley: University of California Press.

Miller, Daniel. 1995. *Acknowledging Consumption: A Review of New Studies*. New York: Routledge.

———. 1998. *A Theory of Shopping*. Cambridge: Polity Press.

Morris, Edward. 2005. *An Unexpected Minority: White Kids in an Urban School*. New Brunswick, NJ: Rutgers University Press, forthcoming.

National Association for the Advancement of Colored People. 2003. "Retail Industry Receives 'D' Grade for Diversity." July 15. Retrieved December 9, 2003, from www.naacp.org/news/2003/2003-07-15-3.html.

Nevaer, Louis. 2001. *Into—and out of—the Gap: A Cautionary Account of an American Retailer*. Westport, CT: Quorum Books.

Newman, Katherine S. 1999. *No Shame in My Game*. New York: Knopf.

Nordquist, Nick. 2003. "Bigger Boxes: The Battle over America's Superstores." KPBS-TV (San Diego, CA). Transcript retrieved March 22, 2005, from www.bigboxtv.com/transcript.html.

Norton, Ann. 1993. *Republic of Signs: Liberal Theory and American Popular Culture*. Chicago: University of Chicago Press.

Ortega, Bob. 1998. *In Sam We Trust: The Untold Story of Sam Walton and How Wal-Mart Is Devouring America*. New York: Random House.

Pristin, Terry. 2004. "Merger Seen as Sign That Outlet Malls Are Not Just a Niche." *New York Times*, October 13, C6.

Project on Disney. 1995. *Inside the Mouse*. Durham, NC: Duke University Press.

Pugh, Allison. 2003. "Where Caring and Buying Meet: On Childrearing, Consumption and Relationship." Paper presented at the annual meeting of the American Sociological Association, Atlanta, GA.

———. 2004. "Windfall Child Rearing: Low-Income Care and Consumption." *Journal of Consumer Culture* 4(2): 229–49.

———. 2005. "Selling Compromise: Toys, Motherhood and the Cultural Deal." *Gender & Society* 19: In press.

Radway, Janice. 1984. *Reading the Romance*. Chapel Hill: University of North Carolina Press.

Rand, Erica. 1995. *Barbie's Queer Accessories*. Durham, NC: Duke University Press.

Raucher, Alan R. 1991. "Dime Store Chains: The Making of Organization Men, 1880–1940." *Business History Review* 65 (Spring):
130–63.

Reskin, Barbara, and Patricia Roos. 1990. *Job Queues, Gender Queues.*
Philadelphia: Temple University Press.

Riesman, David. 1953. *The Lonely Crowd.* Garden City, NY: Doubleday.

Ritzer, George. 1999. *Enchanting a Disenchanted World: Revolutionizing the
Means of Consumption.* Thousand Oaks, CA: Pine Forge Press.

———. 2002. *McDonaldization: The Reader.* Thousand Oaks, CA: Pine
Forge Press.

Robinson, Olive. 1995. "Employment in Services: Perspectives on Part-
Time Employment Growth in North America." In *Retail Employment,*
ed. Gary Akehurst and Nicholas Alexander. London: Frank Cass.

Rollins, Judith. 1985. *Between Women: Domestics and Their Employers.*
Philadelphia: Temple University Press.

Rudy, Preston. 2004. "'Justice for Janitors,' not 'Compensation for Cus-
todians': The Political Context and Organizing in San Jose and Sacra-
mento." In *Rebuilding Labor: Organizing and Organizers in the New
Union Movement,* ed. Ruth Milkman and Kim Voss, 133–49. Ithaca,
NY: Cornell University Press.

Salzinger, Leslie. 2000. "Manufacturing Sexual Subjects: 'Harassment,'
Desire and Discipline on a Maquiladora Shop Floor." *Ethnography*
1(1): 67–92.

———. 2003. *Genders in Production: Making Workers in Mexico's Global
Factories.* Berkeley: University of California Press.

Sandikci, Ozlem, and Douglas Holt. 1998. "Malling Society: Mall Con-
sumption Practices and the Future of Public Space." In *Servicescapes:
The Concept of Place in Contemporary Markets,* ed. John Sherry, 305–36.
Lincolnwood, IL: NTC Business Books.

Schlosser, Eric. 2001. *Fast Food Nation: The Dark Side of the All-American
Meal.* Boston: Houghton Mifflin.

Schor, Juliet. 1998. *The Overspent American: Why We Want What We
Don't Need.* New York: HarperPerennial.

——. 2004. *Born to Buy: The Commercialized Child and the New Consumer Culture*. New York: Scribner.

——. 2005. "Work, Family and Children's Consumer Culture." In *Unfinished Work: Building Equality and Democracy in an Era of Working Families*, ed. Jody Heymann and Christopher Beem, 285–305. New York: New Press.

Schultz, Vicki. 1998. "Reconceptualizing Sexual Harassment." *Yale Law Journal* 107 (April): 1683–1805.

Seiter, Ellen. 1993. *Sold Separately: Children and Parents in Consumer Culture*. New Brunswick, NJ: Rutgers University Press.

Smelser, Neil. 1998. "The Rational and the Ambivalent in the Social Sciences." In *The Social Edges of Psychoanalysis*, ed. N. J. Smelser, 111–24. Berkeley: University of California Press.

Smith, Amy. 2003. "No Deals (Yet) at Wal-Mart." *Austin Chronicle*, September 26, 2003, 23.

Steen, Margaret. 2003. "Container Store's Focus on Training a Strong Appeal to Employees." *San Jose Mercury News*, November 13.

Sternheimer, Karen. 2003. *It's Not the Media: The Truth about Pop Culture's Influence on Children*. Boulder, CO: Westview Press.

Swartz, David. 1997. *Culture and Power: The Sociology of Pierre Bourdieu*. Chicago: University of Chicago Press.

Talwar, Jennifer Parker. 2002. *Fast Food, Fast Track: Immigrants, Big Business, and the American Dream*. Boulder, CO: Westview Press.

Tilly, Chris. 1996. *Half a Job: Bad and Good Part-Time Jobs in a Changing Labor Market*. Philadelphia: Temple University Press.

U.S. Bureau of Labor Statistics. 2002. "Median Usual Weekly Earnings of Full-Time Wage and Salary Workers by Detailed Occupation and Sex." Retrieved December 9, 2003, from ftp.bls.gov/pub/special.requests/lf/aat39.txt.

——. 2003. "Household Data Annual Averages. 39. Median Weekly Earnings of Full-Time Wage and Salary Workers by Detailed Occupation and Sex." Retrieved March 22, 2005, from www.bls.gov/cps/cpsaat39.pdf.

——. 2004. "Household Data Annual Averages. 18. Employed Persons by Detailed Industry, Sex, Race, and Hispanic or Latino Ethnicity." Retrieved April 6, 2005, from www.bls.gov/cps/cpsaat18.pdf.

———. 2005. "Job Openings and Labor Turnover Survey." Retrieved April 4, 2005, from www.bls.gov/jlt/home.htm.

Weems, Robert E. 1998. *Desegregating the Dollar: African American Consumerism in the Twentieth Century.* New York: New York University Press.

West, Candace, and Don Zimmerman. 1987. "Doing Gender." *Gender & Society* 1: 125–51.

Williams, Christine L. 1989. *Gender Differences at Work: Women and Men in Nontraditional Occupations.* Berkeley: University of California Press.

———. 1995. *Still a Man's World: Men Who Do "Women's Work."* Berkeley: University of California Press.

———. 2002. "Sexual Harassment and Sadomasochism." *Hypatia: Journal of Feminist Philosophy* 17 (Spring): 99–117.

———. 2003. "Sexual Harassment and Human Rights Law in New Zealand." *Journal of Human Rights* 2 (December): 573–84.

Williams, Jerome D. 2004. "Perspectives from the Classroom." Paper presented at the Consumer Racial Profiling Conference, University of Texas, Austin, March 30.

Williams, Jerome D., Geraldine Henderson, and Anne-Marie Harris. 2001. "Consumer Racial Profiling: Bigotry Goes to Market." *New Crisis* 108 (November–December): 22.

Willis, Susan. 1991. *A Primer for Daily Life.* London: Routledge.

Worthy, James C. 1984. *Shaping an American Institution: Robert E. Wood and Sears, Roebuck.* Urbana: University of Illinois Press.

Wrigley, Julia. 1995. *Other People's Children.* New York: Basic Books.

Zabin, Carol, Arindrajit Dube, and Ken Jacobs. 2004. "The Hidden Public Costs of Low-Wage Jobs in California." White paper, Center for Labor Research and Education, University of California, Berkeley. Retrieved March 22, 2005, from http://laborcenter.berkeley.edu/livingwage/workingpoor.pdf.

Zelizer, Viviana. 1985. *Pricing the Priceless Child: The Changing Value of Children.* New York: Basic Books.

———. 2002. "Kids and Commerce." *Childhood* 9 (November): 375–96.

———. 2004. "Circuits of Commerce." In *Self, Social Structure, and Beliefs: Explorations in Sociology,* ed. Jeffrey Alexander, Gary Marx, and Christine Williams, 122–44. Berkeley: University of California Press.

INDEX

Abercrombie & Fitch, 55
abusive customers, 85, 196
accelerated depreciation, 25–26
accounting and children, 21,
    145–46, 152–53
Acker, Joan, 54
activism. *See* consumer activism;
    worker-consumer activism
actors, out-of-work, 19, 70
ACT UP, 46
Adbusters, 46
Addams, Jane, 5, 213nn3–4
adulterated contents, 35
advanced degrees, retail workers
    with, 18–19
advertising campaigns: and corpo-
    rate culture, 98, 100–101, 103;
    and marketing toys to children,
    33, 39–47, 104–05, 168, 181,
    216n8; and self-service, 34; and
    worker-consumer activism, 196
affection for children, 150–51, 167,
    177–79, 181–82, 221nn5–6
"affluenza," 15, 187
African American customers: and
    breakdown of interaction rules,
    127–32; and consumer racial
    profiling, 200–203; and cultural
    legitimation, 141–43; at Dia-
    mond Toys, 163–64; and history
    of racial exclusion, 36; and
    identity shopping, 169, 171,
    202–03; and invitation to
    church, 134–35; and matrix of
    domination, 96; neighborhood
    children as, 159–61; and resis-

tance, 14–15; and shop-floor
    culture, 108, 111
African American retail workers:
    and breakdown of interaction
    rules, 122–24, 129–30, 204; at
    Diamond Toys, 50–51, 163; and
    history of racial exclusion,
    36–37, 56, 216n7, 217–18n3;
    hours, benefits, and wages of,
    75; and matrix of domination,
    96; and shop-floor culture, 111,
    113–14, 117, 119–22; and strati-
    fied selling, 19, 52–53, 55–56,
    59, 61–64; and worker-
    consumer activism, 195–96
age differences, 8, 35, 53, 122, 193
aid to families with dependent chil-
    dren, 71
Ailawadi, Kusum L., 214n2
Air Force families, 214n1
airline industry, 30, 94–95, 204
alarms, 59–60
Alger, Horatio, 79
alienation, 12, 65, 188
alliance of workers and consumers,
    21, 211
all-male preserves, 63–64
ambivalence, 13, 175–76, 181,
    222n7
American Journal of Sociology, 6
American-made products, 209–10
American Psychological Association
    (APA), 45
Americans with Disabilities Act,
    200
Andrews, Cecile, 15

DESIGNER: Victoria Kuskowski

COMPOSITOR: Binghamton Valley Composition

INDEXER: Sharon Sweeney

TEXT: 10/15 Janson

DISPLAY: Knockout

PRINTER AND BINDER: Maple-Vail Manufacturing Group